S0-AKO-553

AMERICA GETS MADD!

by Micky Sadoff

Copyright 1990
Mothers Against Drunk Driving®

ALL RIGHTS RESERVED

TABLE OF CONTENTS

ACKNOWLEDGEMENTS

There are many people whose support and contributions not only played a critical role in this book but, more important, in the effort to put an end to the tragedy of drunk driving in America today.

Absolutely essential to both those efforts is Janice Harris Lord, MADD's Director of Victim Services and a nationally-respected leader in the fight for victims' rights.

Gratitude is also expressed to Frances Carroll who wrote the first draft of many of the victim stories included in the book, and to Michael P. Hickey for his editorial assistance.

Most of all, a very special thank you to all those individuals and their families whose stories are featured in this book. More than anyone else, you are the real story of Mothers Against Drunk Driving and our mission to end drunk driving.

Thank you all for sharing your heartache—and your courage—with us.

FOREWORD

(*Ed. note:* The following article by MADD National President Micky Sadoff helps provide insight into this book's author, her family and her dedication to MADD.)

I am not on crutches. I am not in a wheelchair. I do not have brain damage. I see, hear, feel and think as well as ever. In fact, I have no remaining visible injuries. But I do bear the scars inside as the victim of a drunk driving crash, one of the 500,000 victims injured annually.

On January 16, 1982, my husband, Ron and I were hit head-on by a pick-up truck driven by a repeat-offender drunk driver. We had been to dinner with another couple, and the four of us, all parents of small children, were returning home. My husband almost died from his injuries and our friends spent several weeks in the hospital with their injuries. Watching them suffer, as I coped with my own injuries, was incredibly difficult. I am still haunted by the thought of what might have become of our children if all of us had been killed.

I remember well the physical pain and the emotional roller-coaster I seemed to be riding. I remember much of the crash itself as well as the thoughts and frightening emotions which haunted me for months. Perhaps the saddest change of all was saying good-bye to my belief that life was good and fair and just. I know now that the world is not a safe place.

Because I experienced first-hand the devastation that drunk drivers cause, I felt compelled to do something about it. I started the S.E. Wisconsin Chapter of MADD in late 1982.

Our chapter was two months old when our court case was heard in January, 1983. My friends in MADD supported us, wrote letters, and were in the courtroom for us. The trial lasted four days and the offender received the stiffest sentence that I am aware of to date—four and one half years—for injury caused by operating a motor vehicle while intoxicated. I firmly believe that if MADD had not been there, the sentence would have been much more lenient.

I have been particularly committed to highlighting the injured victim experience during my term as president. I understand that taking on an activist role in MADD may be difficult for many injured victims who must utilize all their physical and emotional energy just to keep going. But I know all too well how much they care, because so many of them are forced to remember every time they look in the mirror or try to cross the street.

I am grateful to MADD for all it has done for me and my family. I am grateful to the men and women in my chapter, in my state, and throughout the United States who believe in our message not to drink and drive, and who have said, "Enough!" I am grateful for the youth of America who have looked around at the death and injury they see all too often and said "Enough!" I am grateful to be a part of a movement that continually gains momentum in saying, "Enough."

Introduction

Mothers Against Drunk Driving got its start in 1980 when a 13-year-old girl was killed by a hit-and-run drunk driver.

The driver had been involved in another hit-and-run drunk driving incident just two days earlier and was free on bail!

The child's mother was not only devastated by her daughter's death but outraged when she learned that nothing had been done to keep the offender off the streets.

What started as a campaign by a handful of committed women to save other children from death and other parents from pain became a grass-roots revolution that has evolved today into an organization of thousands of volunteers in hundreds of chapters nationwide. Canada has 13 affiliates, and there are active chapters in New Zealand, Australia and Great Britain as well.

That small crusade is now a non-profit organization with over 2.8 million members and supporters. MADD has stirred the national conscience and involved the American people in a way never before dreamed possible.

The primary reason for MADD's growth and visibility is twofold. First, the ongoing tragedy of drunk driving continues to take thousands of lives and destroy thousands of families each and every year. Second,

MADD works!

Since 1980, more than 1,000 drunk driving laws and more than 1,000 victim rights laws have been enacted nationwide. The rights of victims and survivors of alcohol-related crashes are now being viewed more equitably in a criminal justice system which, just a few years ago, made the rights of the intoxicated driver a priority. Youth programs affiliated with MADD have sprung up in almost every state, providing teenagers with a sound background in alcohol awareness and education.

Best of all, however, all those efforts are saving lives. In 1980, 28,000 Americans were killed by drunk drivers. By 1988, that number was down to 23,352, while the number of miles driven steadily escalated.

That means that each and every day, 12 fewer sons and daughters, moms and dads, sisters, brothers and friends are lost to drunk drivers!

Obviously, the battle is far from over. No matter how many lives we've been able to save, it's hard to claim victory when another American is still killed by a drunk driver every 23 minutes!

And then there are the injuries. 500,000 each year, one a minute! Limbs crushed, bodies broken, helpless innocent people of all ages find their lives destroyed, their dreams shattered—because someone drank too much and committed the crime of getting behind the wheel of a car.

Unless something is done, two out of every five families in America will be involved in a drunk driving crash during their lifetime.

That's why MADD will continue—must continue—its fight for tougher laws, like suspension of drunk drivers' licenses at the time of arrest; confiscation of habitual offenders' license plates; mandatory imprisonment for repeat offenders; lower legal blood alcohol levels, and more.

We cannot relax in that fight, even for a moment, not as individuals, not as a group, and not as a nation. Because none of us is safe. Even though we don't like to think about it, there's no escaping it — you could well be the next innocent victim of a drunk driver.

However, the reverse of that is equally true and inescapable — you could also be the one who keeps that drunk driver off the road.

This book offers a look at some of the men and women — folks just like you — who have faced the incredible tragedy and grief of losing a loved one to a drunk driver, and then channeled that grief into positive, productive programs to try and keep others from suffering similar tragic, needless, losses.

We will examine their stories and we will examine the nationwide efforts developed to prevent those stories from being repeated.

Drunk and drugged driving is a tragedy which will come to an end only if all Americans join together for that purpose.

A Voice for the Victims

MADD's Mission
"The Mission of Mothers Against Drunk Driving
is to stop drunk driving and to support the victims
of this violent crime."

Drunk driving is the most frequently committed
violent crime in America, with more than three times
the number of arrests for all other violent crimes
(murder, forcible rape, robbery and aggravated assault)
<u>combined</u>. That's not to mention that only one of every
2,000 people who drive drunk is arrested.

Service to the victims of drunk driving is at the very
heart of Mothers Against Drunk Driving, as is evidenced by the Mission Statement shown above.

Drunk driving is not an issue of financial costs, ex-
penditure of public resources, violation of public
statute or even of moral principle, although it involves
all these things.

Drunk driving is, ultimately, an issue of human loss,
made all the more tragic by its prevalence.

Sometimes it's too easy to talk about drunk driving
victims in numbers, as we often do. Like the more than
23,000 people killed each year by drunk drivers or the
500,000 people who suffer injuries.

But each one of those is a unique and irreplaceable
individual with a name, a family and dreams which
must now go unfulfilled. Each represents far more than

a faceless number to his or her family and friends, who are now caught in the tragic ripple effect set off by each crash.

It is vital to remember that each drunk driving tragedy affects more than those who are killed or injured in the crash. Their loved ones become victims, too.

As an organization, MADD recognizes its fundamental responsibility to give those victims a voice— both to acknowledge the reality of their loss and to bring that reality to a society all too often benumbed by statistics.

Among the services MADD offers to ease the suffering—the grief, the anger, the confusion—of drunk driving victims are the following.

Crisis Intervention. Alcohol and other drug-related crashes create a critical period in the lives of victims. In order to assist those who have been victimized, MADD chapters provide emotional support to help victims cope with their grief and anger. In addition, victims receive practical information, through 10 different brochures and two books, to help them understand the grieving process and their pending court cases.

Victim Support. MADD brings together those who have been victimized by alcohol and other drug-related crashes to discuss their feelings and their futures on an ongoing basis. Victims can offer each other a unique understanding, providing emotional support and reassurance as they share the loss or serious injury of a loved one. Most MADD Chapters offer victim support groups at no cost to the victim family.

Victim Advocacy. Victims are offered a thorough explanation of the criminal judicial process. MADD advocates clarify the victims' rights, accompany them to court when necessary, and follow up on the sentencing of the offender.

Victim Advocacy Training. In a survey of over 400 victim families a few years ago, 95 percent wished to help other families who had been likewise victimized. In order to facilitate this, MADD offers 40-hour Victim Assistance Institutes to train hundreds of victim advocates each year.

Victim Impact Panels. As victims move through grieving and begin to recover from the powerlessness they felt when the crash happened, many wish to tell their story so that others who might consider drinking and driving will be moved to make a commitment not to do so. About one-third of the chapters bring together three or four victims to tell their stories as a panel before the most important audience who could ever hear them—convicted drunk drivers ordered by the court to attend.

The victims on the panel do not blame or judge those who attend. They simply tell their stories and how their lives and families have been affected by the crash. Victims never speak to groups in which their own offender is present. There is no interaction between victims and offenders during the Panel presentation, but question and answer periods may follow.

Judges or probation officers require convicted drunk driving offenders to attend a Victim Impact Panel as an element of their sentences. The Panel does not replace conventional sentencing but adds a creative component to it. Immediately after the sentence is pronounced, a court clerk informs the offender verbally and in writing of the date, time and place of the Panel to be attended. A probation officer or other agent of the court attends each Victim Impact Panel to monitor attendance. Offenders who fail to attend must return to court for appropriate sanction.

Follow-up research is just beginning on the panels and it looks very promising. In a study of 94 offenders who attended a panel in Dallas, Texas, 87 percent said before attending the panel that they would continue to drink and drive or were unsure. After hearing the panel, 95% said they would never drink and drive again. A large study in Clackamas County, Oregon, followed up 1,275 offenders for one year. 534 of them had been ordered to attend a Victim Impact Panel, 741 were not. The group who did not attend the panel had three times as many drunk driving offenses within the next year as the non-panel offenders.

Public Policy Activism. MADD at the state and national level provides an opportunity for victims and other concerned activists to channel their suffering into pressing for DWI laws which will better protect us against the impaired driver.

A Letter to My Daughter

Others besides judges have seen the benefit of bringing offenders face to face with the emotional story of a drunk driving victim. June Taylor, the founder of MADD's Southwestern Ohio Chapter, wrote this letter to her daughter Julie six years after Julie was killed by a drunk driver. The editor of an Ohio newspaper published it and suggested that judges should require drinking drivers to read June's letter to Julie. "It may succeed where all else fails," he said.

Hi Babe:

Six years ago this week, you were killed by a drunk driver. Since you were in my thoughts when I first opened my eyes today, I decided to sit down and share those thoughts with you, to let you know some of the things that have happened in those six years.

I guess the first thing I should say is how much we miss you. Every day I think of you.

You would be twenty-three now, and I think of what it would be like if you were married, with a child, and could stop in and visit. I wonder what you would look like, whether you would have gone on to college. I suppose one advantage of your dying when you were only seventeen is that you will always be the happy, cheerful cheeky seventeen-year-old that we all remember.

The man who killed you lives nearby. I see him every so often and it still hurts to see him standing in the sunshine, knowing just a few blocks away in Venice Cemetery, your beautiful body is lying in the cold soil, put there because he decided to drive while he was drinking.

Karen and Dudley both survived the crash, mainly because when you saw the drunk driving toward you on your side of the road, you managed to get all four wheels off the road.

You would have been amazed how many people came to your funeral. Our little church was overflowing. You had lots of beautiful flowers and some really unusual memorials.

There is also a television show called "All for the Love of Julie" which is about my starting a MADD chapter after your death. It won several Emmy Awards and was aired nationally. When the producers received their Emmys, one raised the award and said, "Julie, this is for you."

Remember, you had been to see Kenny Rogers the night before you were killed? Well, I wrote to him and told him what had happened to you and asked him to make a statement about drinking and driving. Would you believe he sent a $1,000 check to go in a memorial fund that we have set up in your name?

I see lots of your friends still. Suzi is pregnant now. She has finished college and is doing well in computers. Karen has a little girl. Sheila had a girl, too.

In fact, there was a small ceramic statue of a baby that you were working on when you were killed that I assumed was for her, so I finished it and gave it to her after her child was born. We also finished all the lovely gifts that you were working on for Christmas for us and put them under the Christmas tree.

We still have a lot of things throughout the house that you made. It's rough sometimes because they are a constant reminder of you, but we are proud of how talented you were and try not to remember the horrible way you died.

Remember Christmas 1980? It was the last Christmas that you were alive. You and I were in England because Granddad had both his legs amputated and we had gone there to spend Christmas with him. Looking back, I am so glad that we had that time together in England. Remember when we went out Christmas caroling with the church? What about the Christmas service at St. Paul's Cathedral? Shopping at Harrods? The stockings we made for each other because all of our Christmas presents were in the States?

Sue and Dennis both got married three years ago. Sue and Bob were married in Chicago. Dennis and Pam were married in Forest Park at Forest Chapel. I think you would like Pam. She works with me at MADD. In fact, we have the MADD office in what used to be your bedroom. I felt that you would enjoy all this work to save lives being done in your old room.

Do you remember Lisa? She won a Gold Congressional Medal for her work with SADD (Students Against Driving Drunk). She and I went to Washington, D.C., where she received her award. We went to the White House, Congress, International Press Club and the Vietnam Memorial. We really did it up right.

We have three dogs now. We have a shepherd named Mollie. And, we still have Duchess and Blackie. I used to walk to the cemetery each day with Duchess and Blackie and they seem to know that it is where you are. In fact, Duchess used to sit with me when I would go to your room and cry. I think Blackie used to go to the cemetery sometimes by himself at night, because lots of times, when there was new snow on the ground, I would see dog prints leading to your grave and an imprint where a dog had laid in the snow.

The tree you planted in the back yard is one of the largest in the yard now. Each spring I go out and watch the new leaves coming out and remember Natorp's Garden Shop giving you that little "twig" when you were twelve. We enjoy our breakfast in the shade of it each morning, and we enjoy our afternoon tea under it, too.

"Oktoberfest" has just passed. The last photo we have of you alive was in front of the fountain on Fountain Square. You, your boyfriend, Dad and I had gone down there together for "Oktoberfest."

There is a wooden cross at the side of the road on Route 27 where you were killed. In fact, there are about 100 wooden crosses on "27" where someone has died.

Every time I drive by, I look at where you were killed and start the "what if" scenario. I know it doesn't help, but it's hard not to. "What if" you wouldn't have had tickets for Kenny Rogers? Then you probably would have gone to Chattanooga, Tennessee, with us and wouldn't have been at that spot that night. "What if," "what if," "what if" . . . it is endless and doesn't accomplish anything and just makes the pain worse.

I wish you were here. I wish the pain would go away. Dad and I love you very much. I will be seeing you sometime in the future. Until then, watch over us.

Love,
Mom

Value for Victims, too

A special appeal of Victim Impact Panels is that they have value both for the offenders and for the victims.

If the victims' stories are told in person from the heart, in neither a blaming or accusatory way, they can enable offenders, perhaps for the first time, to consider the pain and suffering drunk driving can cause to other people; help offenders move beyond being "stuck" in focusing on their own "bad luck"; serve as a first step in breaking down denial of alcoholics or those addicted to other drugs; imprint images of real people in offenders' minds which they may replay when drinking and driving is again an option; and change behavior and save lives.

For the victims, the value is that, by giving words to their experiences and feelings, they don't feel as helpless in the aftermath of their experience. One of the most devastating components of crime victimization is its randomness. Victims of drunk driving didn't ask for what happened to them. They certainly never expected it to happen to them . . . only to other people.

Because it did happen to them, much of their old world view—that good things happen to good people and bad things happen to bad people—has been destroyed. They can feel helpless and powerless, almost expecting more bad things to happen to them.

If they are not allowed to participate in the criminal justice system, their sense of powerlessness is enhanced. They can become disillusioned with the criminal justice system when they realize that they are not needed—and sometimes not wanted—in it. Finding some degree of balance and justice in the criminal justice system may be all they have left.

By serving on a Victim Impact Panel, then, they find that the telling of their story lightens their personal pain and promotes their own healing process. They experience something positive from a previously devastating event and they understand that through telling their stories they may be preventing some other family from having to suffer similar victimization.

Says Dawn Phillips of Milwaukee, Wisconsin, after speaking on her first panel, "What a great feeling it is to feel less depressed and more happy today. Could it be because I shared my tragedy with a group of offenders? Will I feel this good every time I do it? I only hope that now they will stop and think before causing another tragedy. If I help even one person, it is great!"

Many Victim Impact Panelists report that, while it is emotionally draining for them to relive and tell their stories, they are strengthened each time they do it. Some have said that participating on a panel helped them move from focusing on the past to cherishing the present and the future, and begin to take charge of their lives once again.

Of course, the greatest service anyone can render to the victims of drunk driving is to do everything in their power to keep others from becoming victims, too.

Victims Have Rights.

MADD has long been a national leader in the drive for statutory Bills of Rights to ensure that victims of alcohol and other drug-related crashes have guaranteed rights within the criminal justice system. For too many years, only the defendant had rights as outlined in the state and federal constitutions, but it is increasingly recognized that the victim must also be accorded such pro-

tections as the right to describe the impact of the crime
on his or her life and to be notified of all steps in the
criminal justice process.

All states now have some victim rights statutes and 48
states have comprehensive Victim Bills of Rights. The
next wave of public policy agenda is to get victims'
rights into state constitutions alongside defendants'
rights. By March, 1990, that goal had been achieved in
five states and amendments were pending in several
others.

A key component of constitutional rights for victims
is allowing the victims to remain in the courtroom during the trial . . . just as the defendants do.

Where is Justice?

You may ask, Don't victims already have the rights
to attend the trials of those who killed their loved ones?
Ask Mary Mitchell, whose two children, Gayla and
Bart, were killed by a drunk driver.

Gayla was 7 and Bart 5 the day they were riding in
the car with their mom and dad, Mary and Ray Mitchell.

A pickup truck with a young drunk driver at the
wheel ran a red light at about 80 miles an hour, hit a
bump, flew 100 feet through the air and smashed into
the Mitchells' car, killing Gayla and Bart and leaving
Ray near death in intensive care.

Mary somehow survived the crash and the sub-
sequent agony of burying her two children alone, while
her husband clung to life in the hospital. Yet in a way,
her victimization had just begun.

When Mary called the District Attorney's office, she
was made to feel like a nuisance for wanting to know

about the prosecution of the man who killed her children, for wanting to give her statement about the crash!

She learned through the newspaper that charges had been filed and that, after numerous delays, the trial had at last been scheduled. She thought maybe then she'd get to be part of the criminal justice system. But once again, she was denied.

The defense attorney subpoenaed her—and then barred her from the courtroom so her presence "wouldn't prejudice the jury." Photographs of her children were not introduced as evidence for the same reason.

The young man who had been driving the pickup truck was found guilty but, prior to sentencing, a host of witnesses paraded to the stand to praise his character and to beg for leniency.

While that was going on, Mary was still not allowed to enter the courtroom or speak about the character of her children or her husband—because "that might prejudice the jury."

After brief deliberation, the jury sentenced the offender to three years' probation. Then two of the jurors embraced the defendant and his mother.

Mary Mitchell learned the hard way, as so many other drunk driving victims have learned, that while criminals are guaranteed dozens of rights, she, as a victim, had none.

As long ago as 1982, the President's Task Force on Victims of Crime had this to say about America's system of criminal justice:

"A judicial system that fails to be equitable cannot survive. America's system was designed to be the fairest in history, but it has lost the balance that was the cornerstone of its wisdom.''

As Mary Mitchell's case pointed out, our system is heavily weighted in favor of the criminal, often at the expense of the victim.

Criminal defendants may receive a court appointed attorney, may elect a trial before a judge or jury, may demand a speedy trial, may confront their accusers, and may choose to be present through the entire trial. Defendants may appeal a court's decision. Generally, the victim has no such rights.

However, thanks to MADD and other victim groups, a state constitutional amendment for victim rights was passed in Mary's state in 1989, and, if her tragedy were to happen today, she would very likely be allowed to attend the trial.

Beyond the Criminal Courtroom

Frustration with the courts does not end in the criminal arena. Many victims also face years of humiliation as they seek to obtain fair outcomes from insurance companies and civil courts.

Rodney and Marie Fetter of Reading, Pennsylvania know that all too well.

When they learned their 18-year-old son Robert had been killed by a drunk driver on April 15, 1983, they knew they were facing the worst pain any parent can endure.

The 29-year-old man responsible for Robert's death had been drinking when he ran the red light and smashed into Robert's car.

He was originally sentenced to a minimum of three years in prison, after a criminal trial that lasted five days. The legal system, however, waited three more years before putting the drunk driver in jail, thanks to a prolonged appeal process.

This delay was one of many problems encountered by the Fetters in their quest for justice in Robert's death. The civil case was not resolved until June, 1989, more than six years after Robert had been killed.

Rodney and Marie Fetter testified at the civil trial. Marie described the experience:

> Testifying was one of the most awful things my husband and I had to contend with since our son's death. Both of us were required to explain how we raised our boy. It hurt to have to defend our parenting skills even though we knew we had done nothing wrong and should not have had to explain a thing.

> Throughout all the trials, there were moments when a normal citizen would have difficulty identifying who the guilty party was in Robert's death, even though the facts and the cause were clear. The defense attorney did everything he could to make the offender look good and tried desperately to make us look like unfit parents. No mention of drunk driving was allowed during the civil trial and the defendant was described as almost innocent because he had decided to plead guilty to his charges. The jury was not allowed to know he was still appealing his conviction in the criminal case.

> The defense attorney also stated that we were all in the courtroom only because a settlement could not be reached, implying that we were asking for an unreasonable amount of money. Never

did he mention the unfair settlements the insurance company had offered us. He told the jury, "This is not a lottery, and the settlement should not entitle the Fetters to a Rolls Royce, furs or diamonds." My husband and I were stunned and extremely hurt. We had not sought a specific dollar figure, only that we receive fair and decent treatment for what we had endured.

The civil trial lasted for four days in 1986, but it was not until June 1989 that the State Superior Court finally ruled that the Berks County Judge properly added $98,500 in delay damages to a civil judgement. The three judge appellate panel said the Judge was correct in adding this amount to the original amount set by the jury verdict in the December 1986 trial, since the insurance company had never in four years seriously attempted to settle the case fairly.

What happened to the Fetters is not about settlements and money. It is about what happens to innocent victims who demand that the justice system act properly. The Fetters endured considerable hardship, humiliation, hurt, stress and pain. But they were determined that the death of their son would not become just another case, rushed through court, with justice overlooked.

Just like the judicial system, insurance companies must deal with victims fairly. Someone has to pay when there is a life snuffed out in a drunk driving crash, and it is only as we stand strong and determined that we will see results.

National Candlelight Vigil

No single event throughout the year focuses more attention on the victims of drunk driving crashes than the National Candlelight Vigil of Remembrance and Hope held in December every year.

They're designed not only to remember the victims, but to support their families, to alert the nation to the reality of drunk driving, and to express hope for a less violent holiday season.

Popular actress Connie Sellecca once wrote of MADD's Candlelight Vigil . . .

> . . . I am convinced that if every driver in America attended just one Candlelight Vigil, drunk driving would no longer be a major national tragedy.

In concert with the National Candlelight Vigil each December, simultaneous local vigils sponsored by MADD chapters are held all across America.

Victims gather from throughout the country and even from abroad, to remember their loved ones through candlelight, song and spoken word. There are no sermons, political speeches or other activities which distract from focus on the victims.

As one victim said, "The Vigil is sad, but it is so important. It's our way of saying 'We remember you' every December. I wouldn't want to go through the holiday season without it."

While the event is always attended by many media

representatives, the media outreach is secondary to the value of the event for the victims themselves.

And sometimes the media get caught up in the program. That's what happened to Jane Vanderpool, a Minnesota reporter:

It would be useful, I thought, to attend the memorial service at the Capitol since I was working on a story about drunken driving.

I'd written about death and tragedy before and didn't think I'd be affected much by the ceremony staged by MADD. It might make me more sensitive, I thought.

A flutist and violinist were playing a concerto duet as I entered the rotunda that cold December night. As music floated above the quiet murmur of voices, people leaned against the marble pillars that surround the Minnesota Star embedded in a polished marble floor. A spotlight focused on the white and red MADD banner above the podium.

Little white candles held in paper cups flickered against the gray sandstone walls as names were read of victims of drunken drivers.

I doubt anyone could sit through that service and not be convinced people who drive after drinking must be stopped—from killing other people and themselves. You just can't listen to the litany of grief and not be changed. Or at least I couldn't.

Death has never touched my family, and it was sometimes hard for me to empathize with people telling their nightmarish stories. But what I saw was that their pain hasn't faded even though for many of them the death occurred several years ago.

Stories usually began with a telephone call in the middle of the night. Suddenly, someone realized they'd never again see a husband, a wife, a parent, a brother, a sister.

I sat cross-legged on the floor, and tears flowed down my cheeks as I filled my notebook with story after story of senseless death.

Circumstances differed, but the message was the same: They still grieve for the one they loved. They're still angry about that death. They're still concerned enough to stand up and tell the world about it, hoping that it will protect others from similar pain.

"My husband and I were in a campground in Montana during a bike trip from San Francisco when the bad news came," one woman said. "Our 23-year-old son had to tell us that our oldest daughter was dead and another daughter was lying in a hospital after nine hours of surgery."

"The fact that the drunk driver who hit them also killed himself really didn't make it easier," she said.

"My son was killed in a crash," another woman said. "He was a popular, athletic teenager, returning home after drinking at a homecoming party. He drove his car into a ditch"

"I don't have a second party to get angry at," his mother said. "But I do feel angry at a society that says it's OK to drink and drive."

"Many Americans were angry about losing 57,000 men in Vietnam," she said. "Why aren't they angry about the 260,000 people killed by drunken drivers in the same period?"

One man lost three sons in one year—killed in different crashes by different drunken drivers. Another man lost his wife and a daughter in a crash 20 years ago and still mourns their deaths.

"I always wanted to complain. I wanted to scream and shout bloody murder because justice isn't done," he said. His feelings slowly changed. "Drunk drivers don't want to kill people. They need help. We can do something to change this deplorable state of affairs. It doesn't have to go on and on and on."

Dozens of stories were told by what became double rows of mourners around the star on the rotunda floor. Each held a lighted candle. Every few minutes, a bell tolled three times in memory of the dead.

Sometimes drunken drivers themselves are killed, victims of their own lack of judgement. Their deaths are also tragic. They have families, too.

Every day people die because somebody can't keep a car between two white lines.

I wondered what crash victims think as they see a car hurtling toward them. I wondered if they sit frozen in shock and fear, if they realize they're looking at death. Do they ask how this could be happening to them?

I don't know how I could live with myself if I caused a crash that killed someone. I don't ever want to be responsible for putting a crying high school girl at the MADD podium, like the one I saw there.

She burst into tears as she started to tell her story. Her brother and a friend went bar-hopping in Wisconsin last spring, she said, and their car rolled into a ditch on the way home.

Her brother was killed.

"He was a great brother," she sobbed. "I've always felt so cheated . . ."

MADD has a rallying cry, "Murder by car is still murder."

While the Candlelight Vigil is a memorial event, remembering and paying tribute to those who have already been killed by drunk drivers, it is the fervent hope of everyone in attendance that such an event will also call attention to the truth about drinking and driving.

In so doing, perhaps others will be spared the need to gather in December to light a candle and say a prayer for their loved ones lost to drunk drivers.

At Risk: America's Most Precious Resource

Every life lost to drunk driving causes pain and anguish, but nothing causes greater agony than the killing of a child.

"A Part of Our Souls Ripped Away"

Robbie and Jeff Jensen know how much it hurts.

Even though they both had successful careers, they dreamed of the day when they could have a child with whom to share their happiness and their love.

For 13 years they tried, refusing to give up hope even when doctors told them they would never be able to conceive a child.

Their hope paid off. Their dream came true when little Aubrey was born on April 5, 1984. She became the joy of their lives and the apple of their eyes.

With beautiful blond hair, sparkling blue eyes and a warm, sweet, loving personality, Aubrey was the miracle child Robbie and Jeff had prayed for.

By age four, Aubrey loved to listen to Michael Jackson and to dance to his music. Quick to laugh and eager to play, every day brought new experiences and new joys.

With Aubrey in their lives, Robbie and Jeff felt they had everything any family could ever want.

Until June 22, 1988.

Robbie was scheduled to leave town that day on a

business trip, so she left her job early to come home and spend some time with Aubrey before she left.

They cuddled on the couch and Robbie painted Aubrey's toenails while they watched television and just chatted with one another like best friends.

But soon it was time to leave, so Jeff and Aubrey drove Robbie to the airport. Robbie remembers her conversation with Aubrey just before she left. "I had told her that I was really lucky to be her Mom and she was really a special little girl."

That was the last conversation Robbie and her daughter would ever have.

On the way home from the airport, Jeff and Aubrey decided to stop to pick up a few groceries.

They were passing through an intersection when a man who chose to drink and drive ran a red light. He was driving a dump truck and pulling a trailer with a twelve-ton bulldozer on it—unchained.

The Jensens' car was flattened by the bulldozer. Aubrey was killed instantly and Jeff was seriously injured.

When Robbie's plane landed in Atlanta, she was met by an airport official and told to call her brother. He told her there had been an accident. The airline tried to get her back home as soon as possible, but delays and bad weather made it difficult.

Finally, after what seemed like an eternity, her plane touched down. As she left it, she saw her whole family waiting for her at the gate.

And she knew.

"I could tell from the looks on their faces that Aubrey was dead."

She also learned that Jeff was in the hospital with a

severe concussion, punctured lung, broken ribs, lower back damage, neck damage, and bleeding from the kidneys.

Despite the severity of his injuries, Jeff was released from the hospital three days after the crash. As Robbie explained, "We had a funeral to plan. We had to find a place to bury our daughter. We had to plan a service. All these things that we never, ever believed we would be doing, we were having to do."

Robbie's sad eyes and the pain in her voice display an anguish only a mother can fully understand. She's haunted by the fact that "I was not there for my daughter. That was a really difficult thing, to not be there for her or Jeff."

The shock has worn off for the Jensens who now face the harsh reality of living each day without their "miracle child," their beautiful daughter.

It has been very hard for these grieving parents. They are now active in MADD in Minnesota, both in gratitude for the support they have received and in the hope of seeing that Aubrey's death was not in vain.

They've had to adjust every portion of their lives. Jeff's injuries left him unable to work. Robbie could no longer endure working at the same company after Aubrey's death. She found a new job which gave her more time for healing and more time to devote to MADD.

Jeff sums up the tragedy that struck their little family: "We're brokenhearted. We are just not one hundred percent any more. We just feel that a part of our souls was ripped from us. We'll never go a day, or really, any small part of a day, without missing her. It's somewhat like putting a little cup in the ocean and drawing it out to try and tell you about Aubrey. Because her existence, her being here, was the ocean. She was everything to us."

The Grinch

Katie Owen will never go through a Christmas without remembering the pain that came from losing her daughter, Teri, at the hands of a drunk driver:

With the Christmas decorations all in place around town and the sound of holiday music playing, I cannot help but reflect on Christmases past. Could it possibly have been so many years ago that a blond-haired, green-eyed little girl climbed up on my lap and asked, "Mommy, please read me 'How the Grinch Stole Christmas' just one more time." The pages in the story book were frayed from having been turned so many times as once more I read the Christmas story to my little girl.

As I went through the story of how the Grinch stole all the presents that belonged to the children in the little village, I asked my daughter why she liked such a sad story. I remember her innocent little smile as she looked up at me and said, "I'm not worried, Mommy, because I know my Mommy would never allow anyone to steal Christmas." At that time I hugged her and told her she was right. I said I was thankful to have my little girl feel so secure and loved. I was happy she had so much faith in her mother.

The beautiful little girl grew into a young lady and her mother was very proud of all her accomplishments in high school. She was the absolute joy of her family. But then the unthinkable happened. The GRINCH STOLE OUR CHRISTMAS.

Masquerading as a drunk driver, the grinch killed my beloved daughter on August 24, 1985. Like a thief in the night he stole Teri's life and our Christmas forever and ever. She was killed by three boys who were classmates as she was on her way home from a high school football game. Two of the boys had attended the same game and one of them had played in it. Two drank before the game with the player joining in the drinking after the game.

They were grinches the night Teri died because Christmas will never be the same nor will any other day have the same meaning again because of what happened to Teri.

It's unthinkable to know how many drunk drivers who kill innocent victims are safe and secure in their homes during the holiday season. They may even be decorating their tree while just a short distance away, my daughter and other victims lie in the cold graves at the cemetery just because someone chose to drink and drive.

I hope that people will think twice before they get behind the wheel of a car after they've been drinking. Don't take the life of another child. Don't be the grinch that steals another family's Christmas forever.

Yes, America's youngest citizens are very much at risk in our country today. That's why, while many of MADD's programs are aimed at high schoolers, teenagers and young adults, we make special efforts to reach out to younger children as well.

Meredith Baxter Birney once wrote in a letter to MADD supporters of the feelings she had as she watched a school year begin:

There's something special about this time of year as America's children return to school that fills me with joy—and with deep concern.

The joy comes from watching boys and girls of all ages go by and trying to imagine what they're going to be like when they grow up.

How about that little girl over there? With that serious look on her face. Will she be a doctor? A teacher?

That young fellow over there. Will he turn out to be a lawyer? Perhaps a CPA?

In their sweet faces, I can see tomorrow's baseball players, TV newscasters, astronauts, secretaries, carpenters, sales people, and even actors and actresses.

Yet, soon I find my mind no longer focusing on the happy thoughts of career choices to be made in years to come. That's when the concern, the fear, starts.

Because I start thinking about other choices that many of them are facing right now . . . choices that determine not what their future will be but whether or not they will even have a future.

Those choices relate to the use of alcohol or other drugs.

Believe me, our children are being pressured to make those choices at unbelievably young ages.

How young? One survey found that more than

a third of all 4th graders feel peer pressure to drink! 4th graders!

And that pressure obviously has an impact, since the average age at which our young people first use alcohol is 12!

That's why Meredith is a supporter of MADD, especially MADD's programs for young people.

The MADD Poster/Essay Contest

One such program that has grown nationally in popularity and participation every year since it was introduced is MADD's Poster/Essay Contest.

This contest involves students in elementary and middle as well as senior high schools. Participants are rewarded for their efforts and at the same time, their entries call attention to the problem of drinking and driving and the need for greater public awareness of this national tragedy.

The poster competition is open to students in grades 1-12, the essay contest to students in grades 4-12.

The program began in 1987 with 15,000 entries from throughout the country. By 1989, MADD received more than three times that amount, over 45,000 entries.

One reason for the rapid growth is the number of organizations which have helped to promote entries. Among many publications which highlight the contest are *The Elks Magazine, American Teacher, Arts & Activities, Contemporary Pediatrics, Learning '88,* and *Target*.

The contest was also featured in *Encyclopedia Britannica's 1989 Medical and Health Annual.*

Plus, with the addition of Spanish entries in 1989, several Hispanic publications, including *Que Pasa* and

Vista, carried information on the contest.

Support has also come from schools and organizations such as the Farmers Home Administration, Girl Scouts, Boys and Girls Clubs of America and 4-H Clubs.

Perhaps the best way to convey the impact of the MADD Poster/Essay Contest is to simply read some of the essays that have been submitted.

The theme for 1990's contest was "Make This the Decade of Difference—Drive Safe and Sober!"

Larry Conrad Feliciano Segarra of Hormigueros, Puerto Rico, won the Grade 4-6 First Place National award with his essay that told of his dreams and asked adults to let him have a chance to realize those dreams:

"Make This the Decade of Difference.

Drive with Caution and Soundness

of Mind and Body"

I am a child and like all children, I like to dream of beautiful things. Each night I go to bed with the desire to dream; I dream that I will wake up in a country where there are no liquor stores; a country where fathers are not drunks; a country where there are no fights due to alcohol; a country where no beer or rum is sold. But, I feel very sad because I awaken in a country that is not the one of my dreams.

My country is one of the highest in alcohol consumption; also a country where more people die due to alcohol on our streets. In my country the newspapers and the news media only speak of the horrible, bad and ugly things that men do when they are drunk or are under the influence of drugs.

I wish to ask all the adults not to drink and to do wonderful and beautiful things for us, the children. You have the opportunity to make things right so that we can grow to be good and responsible men. If you will help us, someday we will live in the country of my dreams, which every child like myself hopes for.

I invite the government, the doctors, the newspaper media, the owners of liquor stores, and the artists to make a difference. I know that all of us can help not to glamorize the bad and the ugly things and to demonstrate the reality so that children will not become alcoholics or drug addicts.

My teachers and lecturers help me to grow up physically and mentally sound and I will be able to help others. For this reason I feel like shouting . . .

"MAKE THIS THE DECADE OF DIFFERENCE. DRIVE WITH CAUTION AND SOUNDNESS OF MIND AND BODY."

In Grade 7-9, the First Place National Winner, Jeremy Delay of Grants Pass, Oregon, wrote about the crash that nearly took his grandmother's life and left her badly injured:

> "3.59 plus deposit"
> One six pack of beer equals . . .
> $3.59 plus deposit equals . . .
> One night of terror equals . . .
> Lives shattered forever . . .
> $3.59 plus deposit

It was a clear night, July 22nd. The lights of the county fair could be seen in the rear view mirror.

When next my grandfather looked up he saw headlights approaching very fast. He knew they would slow down. But they didn't. They were hit from behind by a black van doing estimated speeds of 100 miles per hour. Shoved from behind their classic 1956 Dodge sheared eight guard rail posts, flipped in mid-air and landed in a field beside the freeway. The freeway was on fire. Their night of terror had just begun.

Headlights. Fire light. Ambulance lights. Emergency room lights. Thousands of dollars and thousands of hours later, my grandmother lived. But the quality of her life had been shattered as easily as her bones were.

We were blessed with a few more years to have her near.

My grandmother rests now where no pain will assail her.

Fond memories mingle with the unanswered question. Would my grandparents have had to suffer through that night of terror if the drunk driver behind the wheel of that black van hadn't paid that initial price of $3.59 plus deposit . . . the cost of a six pack of beer? So, let's have this night of terror not happen again.

Drive safe and sober.

In the Grade 10-12 division, William Burris of Mascoutah, Illinois was the First Place National Winner with his essay entitled simply:

"The Beast"

The beast has run wild since the dawn of time. It has attacked entire families and torn apart whole communities. It has ruined lives around the globe and has been feared by all in one way or another. In recent years its attacks have become even more frequent and much more violent—the beast is now armed. It begins its rampage unaware of the events which will follow, but as time progresses, a metamorphosis occurs creating an uncontrollable taker of lives and breaker of hearts. We search for this menace constantly, always trying to predict its next attack. Unfortunately, it is naked to the human eye in its common form and can be found in all ranks of society. Thus, we await its move, always knowing it could happen, but never quite prepared when it strikes close to home. The beast I speak of is the dangerous, and murderous, drunk driver. During the present decade, however, this mighty beast will fall, banished to the realms of history. For we seek accountability, and we will have justice. We have unified our forces, and we stand strong together. This is no longer a mere battle. It is a war . . . a war for life. Our weapons are knowledge and education; our soldiers, the responsible.

A message to all who drink and drive: Beware, the hunt has begun and there is no longer a place to hide.

Seeing the thought, creativity and effort that America's young people put into their posters and essays, and the powerful messages they get across, makes us hopeful that we may one day have an entire generation of Americans who will not drink and drive.

Other Youth Education Programs

MADD has other national programs to educate

younger Americans to the dangers of driving under the influence of alcohol or other drugs and to help them develop good, safe habits <u>before</u> they begin to drive.

Free for Life

One of those programs, "Free for Life," is a refusal skills development training program to teach junior high school youth how to resist peer and societal pressures to use alcohol and others drugs—pressures that, as we have seen, are felt as early as the fourth grade.

Curiosity, acceptance, lack of self-confidence and pressure to succeed are contributing factors in alcohol and other drug use by students. Developed jointly by MADD and Lifetime Learning Systems, Inc., "Free for Life" addresses each of those factors.

Of special importance, students are helped to recognize and deal with peer pressure and to develop practical refusal skills that can be used to resist that pressure in a variety of difficult situations.

MADD Student Library

In addition, MADD has developed the "Student Library" to meet the needs of countless students who request information about teenage drunk driving.

This invaluable document contains statistics, case studies, creative ideas for student activities, and an extensive bibliography of resources on highway safety issues.

In all its efforts aimed at America's young people, MADD works to develop programs in which the youths are involved as active participants. Such programs are far more effective than "preaching to" or "nagging" young people will ever be.

Most of our youngsters are as frightened of being killed in drunk driving crashes as we, their parents are, that they will be. Together, we work to prevent that tragedy from happening.

Best of all, perhaps by teaching our children something, we can learn something ourselves.

Not long ago, for example, we received a letter from a young father, a man who described himself as someone who rarely drank to excess but who also thought nothing about driving with a cooler in the car and having a beer or two along the way.

Until the day his 7-year-old son looked at him and said, "Daddy, you shouldn't drink and drive. We could get killed."

The father looked at his little boy. "I started to answer him, to explain away the beer in my hand, to tell him it was okay, that this was different."

"But I found I couldn't do it. I realized for the first time, looking into his eyes, that it wasn't different—and it wasn't okay!"

Like far too many Americans, that dad had heard the message, but didn't think it applied to him. Now, thanks to an innocent 7-year-old, he realizes it does.

Fathers Hurt, Too

The loss of a child or any other loved one to a drunk driver is certainly not devastating only to mothers. Fathers hurt, too.

Many of MADD's most active members are men — fathers, brothers, sons or friends of victims of drunk drivers who, while still living with their own grief, are willing to work hard to spare others from suffering as they have.

"He was only a baby, Dad!"

Glenn Birch shared the following thoughts about the death of his 22-month-old son, Courtney. They were spoken at the 1989 Candlelight Vigil as Glenn's surviving son, Rahmlee, stood beside him, holding Courtney's picture.

<u>Yesterday</u> . . . I see it so clearly. As I walk in the door after a long day at work, little Courtney greets me with a hug. He brings me the nerf ball, so I toss it across the room. He laughingly waddles and retrieves it and wants to play some more. He's discovered running at 18 months of age.

No dad could be prouder! After all, he's my son.

Later, his mother and I climb into bed and cuddle close together. We hear little feet running. We giggle. Courtney climbs in on her side and squeezes in the middle. "Move over dad," Lena says, "let my precious in." No woman could have been a better mother for our two sons.

Today . . . We no longer experience the joy we once shared. My son, her precious, was killed on May 3, 1988. He was 22 months young, so full of love, joy and futuristic dreams.

Our pain is shared by his grandmother who was looking after him and the aunt who attempted with all her might to save him. It happened too fast to react. I can never fully know the trauma Lena, my wife, experienced as the helicopter she had been watching as she drove home from work landed at our house as she approached our drive-way. She has never been or never will be the same, since that helicopter took her baby.

Since Courtney died, I have been out of work and have attempted two different jobs. I just could not believe this had happened and could not concentrate.

Our other son, Rahmlee, wishes he were dead instead, not understanding death at all. "He was only a baby, Dad!" How does a father respond to that?

Our entire extended family are victims, as we later discovered, of a senseless death caused by a speeding drunk driver with five previous convictions. He was driving over 60 miles per hour in a 30 miles per hour zone with a blood alcohol content of .26 an hour after the crash — nearly three times the legal limit. No words can describe the pain. A part of ourselves is missing. Now we can only adjust.

As my sorrow turned to anger, I have channeled it into usefulness with the help of MADD. I was determined to make sure this man was held accountable. No one, let alone my baby, should have to lose a life like this. Support from our family and friends, the media, and MADD resulted in a guilty conviction and a 17-year sentence for the offender. He will probably serve about six years. But nothing will ever fill the void in our lives. I will continue to speak out about my son's senseless death in hope that even one person may listen and change.

<u>Tomorrow</u> . . . most of us realize that each person is unique in their grieving, requiring more love, more understanding, more time, more stress outlets than most people think. You never get over the loss. You learn to live with it.

So, I cry when I want to. I sometimes choose not to be strong. I offer my support when I can and may ask for support in return.

I love you yesterday, today and tomorrow, my dear son Courtney Alan Birch. I will relive your memories in all my tomorrows.

Speaking for Jamey

Another grieving Dad, Jim Murray, wrote this story from the perspective of his son, Jamey, while Jamey lay in a coma near death.

It was a beautiful July, 1985 day, and I had helped some friends move. I was feeling good, so I decided to go hop on my bike to train, as I did every day, for a big race I planned to enter in August.

The wind was blowing on my perspiring skin, and the oxygen I breathed in made me feel glad that I was alive. It was warm, the sky was clear, and there was little traffic. I headed for Magazine Mountain to put more stress on my leg muscles and to give me greater lung endurance.

I waved to three people who were loading their hang glider, and they waved back. Friendly folks here in Arkansas, I thought. Suddenly I noticed the sick, weaving motion of a car ahead of me. The stupor of a drunken mind was about to produce a deadly, head-on blow. It would happen faster than the strike of a cobra and would be nearly as deadly.

I froze in terror! My treasured bike was demolished. My helpless body began flipping in space and the last thing I remember was the crushing blow of the car and a deep, deep blackness swallowing me up.

Somewhere out of the darkness I smelled the stench of alcohol as it seethed from the car. Something clogged my throat and I couldn't breathe. My lungs hurt, my leg was broken, and my head . . . what had happened to my head? My brain felt like a bowl of gelatin that had been violently shaken, nerve connectors severed, tissue beaten. Everything was so deep . . . so black.

I faintly recall the sound of cans and bottles being tossed from the car and the hysterical scream, "I'm a murderer. I just killed him!"

Another, calmer voice urged, "Get in the car. Come on, let's go."

Then I felt the gentle hands of my friends with

the hang glider opening my mouth, allowing the blood to flow out. Someone inserted a tube in my throat and finally I sucked in the fresh, warm, life-giving air.

Other gentle hands lifted me, soothed me, and loved me. But over and over came the deep, heavy blackness that would not let go.

Sometimes now I hear the voices of Mom, Dad, sister, brother, grandparents and friends, but for some reason, I can't wake up. I struggle. I try. But I keep falling back into the deep black hole.

The doctors said that if Jamey lived past the first three critical days, there would be the possibility of paralysis and dependence on a life-support system. No one knew the effect of the "extensive brain damage."

Jamey's struggle was long and hard. A month after the collision, he was able to breathe unassisted and had opened his eyes, but remained in a coma. He remained in a coma for another month and remembers very little for the next six months. He could not talk, walk or hold his head up.

Today, Jamey is a living example of what courage, hard work, and prayer can do. Jim, his father, started a MADD chapter in Carthage, Missouri, and has served as State Coordinating Chairperson. Jamey is now able to drive his own pick-up and spends much of his free time writing letters to his old friends from college as well as new ones he has made since his crash.

According to the police report, the driver who hit Jamey was a seventeen-year-old girl who had a blood alcohol content of .16. She had no driver's license. She was sent to "Youth Bridge" in Fayetteville, Arkansas, where she spent ten months. According to their literature, this facility offers "camping and canoeing, sometimes art shows or theatrical productions, arts and crafts and music lessons."

The owner of the car, another young woman, was passed out in a drunken stupor in the front seat of the car. She would serve 30 days in jail with eleven months of her sentence suspended.

Six months later, the owner was again arrested for DWI and then served the eleven month suspended sentence in the Franklin County Jail in Ozark, Arkansas.

Lightning Can Strike Twice — and More!

Just because a family has already been the victim of a drunk driving tragedy doesn't mean they can't be struck again.

Patty and Lou Herzog know all too well that lightning can strike twice.

On New Year's Eve, 1981, their 18-year-old daughter, Susan, was killed by a drunk driver. On May 28, 1987, a second daughter, Debbie, was critically injured by another drunk driver.

Susan was killed in a head-on collision with a 17-year-old drunk driver. The Herzogs asked for the maximum penalty of a year in jail for the youth who took their daughter's life.

Instead, he was ordered to take a year off from school to speak against drinking and driving to community groups. Unfortunately, even that penalty didn't stand and he graduated with his high school class less than six months later.

Patty described the impact of her daughter's death.

On January 1, 1982, a drunk driver killed my youngest daughter, Susan. It was at that point that I began to realize what prolonged grief and sadness were all about. For a long time I was just an observer of life from a distance. Although I wanted to participate in things that were going on, I felt detached from life.

The feeling of sadness is so overwhelming that I don't know why it doesn't kill more people.

Friends try their best to help but actually there is very little that anyone can do to help. Only one thing helps—time. It just takes time to learn to live through this time of sadness and separation. Sleep is the only respite.

Debbie Herzog, 25, had been shopping and was returning home when she was seriously injured in a car crash. She suffered numerous facial injuries, two broken legs, one a compound fracture that doctors said would require up to nine months for recovery, and a broken cheek bone.

"You never think it's going to happen once, but when it happens twice you get a little gun-shy," said Lou Herzog.

The man who hit Debbie was charged with driving while intoxicated, fleeing the scene of an accident involving injuries, and driving with a suspended license.

Less than a week after the wreck, the man posted $200 bail and was out of jail.

The Herzogs were dismayed and upset. "He was out on a lousy $200 bond before Debbie was out of the operating room," stated Patty. "He's out—and she'll be laid up at least six months. There's something wrong with all of that," she added.

The Herzogs' tragedy hit close to home because after Susan's death in 1981, the family became very active in the Northern Virginia MADD Chapter.

Lou has served as MADD Chapter president, chairman of the Virginia State Coordinating Committee and is now a MADD Regional Planning Administrator. Patty chairs the State Victim Assistance program.

Grief-stricken and filled with rage over their daughter's death, this family was determined to channel their feelings into positive action through their work with MADD. They labored tirelessly for tougher state laws, spending countless hours in courts monitoring cases, and in working with victims.

"After we lost Susan, we plunged into working with MADD," Patty said. "Victims Assistance seemed the area where I felt the most qualified to help. Being able to relate exactly with the pain and anger helps me to understand and be patient with all aspects of victims assistance."

That's what made Debbie's terrible crash so much harder to take. As angry as they had been about the lenient sentence given the man who killed their beloved Susan, now they learned that the man who swerved across the center line to smash into Debbie had previous convictions for drunk driving and careless driving!

It took rescue workers two hours to cut Debbie loose from her demolished car. During that endless period of time, she thought a lot about her parents and what had happened to her sister.

"I feel lucky every minute of the day," she said. "I'm alive. If somebody would have told me this would happen two weeks before it did, I'd have said I'll die first. But you can deal with anything. It all depends on how you look at the situation."

Debbie Herzog had to give up her new job to return to Virginia for recovery and rehabilitation from her injuries.

The Herzogs believe strongly that public awareness is a key to saving lives in the drinking and driving issue. "We need to get to our youngsters, in elementary school," Lou said. "By the time they're seniors in high school they won't listen any more," Patty added.

But they also say children aren't the only ones who need education. More often than not, it's the parents who must be taught. And, the Herzogs intend to stay MADD until everyone understands about the dangers of drinking and driving.

"I can't envision our not being involved in MADD," Patty said, "we loved Susan too much and feel this is what we do for her."

Enough is Enough!

Kay Neil could be forgiven if she never rode in a car again. After she became the victim of a drunk driver for the third time, she became active in MADD, organizing the first chapter in Nebraska in 1982.

Here's her story:

In 1950, I had polio which paralyzed almost every part of my body including my speech and most of my breathing ability. With an enormous amount of support from my parents, I survived and was able to walk after two rehabilitation centers and nine months in the hospital.

Then in 1953, my friend and I were hit by the "town drunk." He was never even given a ticket for drunk driving. That was my first taste of being hit by a drunk driver.

The second time came in 1970, when my husband Ed and I were on our way home about one in the morning and were struck by a medical student who was drunk. We were no more than five blocks from the safety of our home when it happened.

The car spun in mid-air and I could see the shattered glass spraying into the air like snowflakes although it was June. It was an eerie sight.

As the car settled to the ground, the silence was like no other silence that I have ever heard. There was no sound, no people, no lights, almost like heaven is supposed to be.

As I began to gather the sights and sounds around me, I recognized that Ed was standing by my side of the car. He was asking me questions. After some confusion, he picked me up and put me in the back seat of the police cruiser. I was quickly whisked away to the emergency room at the hospital only two blocks away.

At the hospital, they removed my brace and discovered no broken bones. But my leg was so painful that they gave my brace to Ed and he put me in the car and we went home. We called my parents and some friends who came to our aid. I had no idea that recovery would take so long, but by August, I was still not able to walk.

Then there were the blackouts, constant and unpredictable. Maneuvering on crutches became impossible because of the blackouts, yet the doctor offered no encouragement that I would ever walk again.

Finally in November, after soaking my foot in gallons of epsom salts water, we managed to get my brace on and I took my first step.

After two court trials and a civil financial settlement, we began to try to put our lives back in order.

The continuing blackouts, due to torn ligaments and sprained muscles at the base of my skull made it impossible for me to work full time, so I began getting into various kinds of volunteer work.

Looking back, I realize how lucky we were in the third crash which happened in April 1981 — not only to have been hit three times and still escape with my life, but because Ed and I were better equipped, knew more what to do, were less afraid of the system. We had definitely learned how to stand up for our rights.

The system works, but it works on behalf of the defendant. The victim is victimized all over again every step of the way. By working with MADD, I'm helping other victims overcome the system's failures.

Fighting the Odds

Ginny Herale has been struck twice by the tragedy of drunk driving, losing a sister, a brother and a niece in the process. But the impact on her family extends far beyond the loss of her siblings and her niece.

I'm from a large family (8 boys, 5 girls). We celebrate the holidays together as a family. On Christmas Eve, 1980, we were all gathered at my parents' house for our Christmas dinner. We had all contributed a dish to the meal.

After a few jokes about my 27-year-old sister being late again, we decided to go ahead and eat since the small children were getting anxious to open presents.

We had barely finished eating when the telephone rang. My mom answered the phone. It was my brother-in-law. He told her, "Mom, we've been in a bad accident, they are all serious but me."

My mom and dad, one brother and one sister, left for the hospital. What they found was that my sister, Cecilia, had been dead on arrival. Four-year-old Jessica was also dead. Six-year-old Jennifer and 20-month-old Justin were both in a coma with skull and other multiple fractures.

My brother-in-law didn't even hold the funeral for five days because he didn't know how many he would have to bury.

The drunk driver who killed my sister and her four-year-old daughter paid a $250 fine and to this day still drinks in the same tavern and brags about how easy he got off. He had a BAC of .289. This occurred just 8 days before the new "tough drunk driving laws" went into effect in Wisconsin.

This tragedy seemed to make our close family even closer. We learned to be even more caring and supportive. We still had my sister's two other children to help through the physical and emotional healing. We had to stay strong for them.

Just as we were starting to heal from this tragedy, it happened again. Less than three years later, my 20-year-old brother, Joey, was killed by another drunk driver. This tore us apart.

We all felt the guilt. Why didn't we do something the first time it happened? Our MADD chapter was just forming in our county. We now found the strength to attend the meetings. Even

though we cried through them, we found the
MADD members were there for us and eventually
we were able to give back some of the healing we
received from these wonderful people.

Joey's death was not the only thing this drunk
driver caused. One of my sisters had to be hos-
pitalized after suffering a psychotic episode. For
several years after, this problem reoccurred near
the anniversary of his death. Plus we watched our
parents age 10 years in a few short months. Their
previous good health is now gone forever.

My parents were so wrapped up in their own
grief and anger they could not tend to the needs
of their children. Finally my younger brother
became involved in counseling and that was the
real turning point.

This time, the drunk driver that killed my
brother received 13 months in the Huber Center.

She was also ordered to pay restitution and to
do community service. That was considered a real
tough sentence. Our family was bitter. We
wanted her to do five years in prison.

The judge allowed her to spend 4 hours a day
with her children and to go to work at night. She
was only at the Huber Center to sleep. What my
mother would give for four hours a day with the
children drunk drivers have taken from her!

Today, my family is so appreciative of the support and help everyone at MADD gave to us and
we hope that through our own involvement, we
can be of help to someone else who goes through
what we are going through.

Yet we face the fact that our family is not

through yet. Statistics predict that two out of every five people alive in the United States today will at some point in their lives be involved in a drunk driving crash.

Out of 13 children, two are already dead. We have at least two more to go, unless we do something about it now. "Do something about it now."

Ginny's statistics are correct. Two out of every five Americans alive today will be involved in an alcohol-related crash at some point in their lives.

Working together, we <u>can</u> do something about it. Now!

America "Ties One On"

In the preceding chapter, Ginny Herale wrote about losing her sister to a drunk driver on Christmas Eve. Patty and Lou Herzog's daughter was killed by a drunk driver on New Year's Eve.

Sad to say, their stories are far from unique or even unusual. In fact, over 10 percent of all those killed in drunk driving crashes in any given year will be killed during the Christmas–New Year's holiday season.

Parties everywhere, frantic last-minute shopping, people traveling near and far to be with relatives or loved ones—a whole host of factors combine to turn one of the happiest times of year into one of the most dangerous.

And, for those who lose a loved one to a drunk driver during this period, those holidays will never be the same again. Instead of feeling joy and celebration, these holidays trigger memories of great sadness and loss.

It was to lower that risk, to reduce that danger, that MADD launched Project Red Ribbon in 1986.

The concept is very simple. Americans are asked to "tie one on for safety" during the holiday period between Thanksgiving Day and New Year's Day by tying a simple red ribbon. They affix it to the door handle on the driver's side of their car or some other visible location on the vehicle. The ribbon serves as a vivid reminder to drive safe and sober during the holidays.

The ribbon is not only a declaration that the owner of that vehicle will drive safely during the holidays, but also a motivator to others who see it to do the same.

None of us, even in our wildest dreams, could have predicted the success Project Red Ribbon would enjoy.

In 1986, more than one million red ribbons were tied on to cars and trucks all across the country!

But as staggering as that figure was, it seems almost minuscule when compared to what has happened with Project Red Ribbon since then.

It has easily become MADD's best known, most visible program. In 1989, an estimated 40 million red ribbons were distributed and used.

Americans put the little red ribbons on cars, trucks and almost any other form of transportation imaginable.

MADD takes pride that more ribbons are seen each year, and many people are keeping their ribbons tied on past the holidays and throughout the whole year.

Red Ribbon Vegas Style

In 1988, Las Vegas, Nevada went all out for Project Red Ribbon. MADD Clark County Chapter Administrator, Sandy Heverly, reported that the entire city was covered with red ribbons during the holidays.

Ribbons were seen on 460 yellow cabs representing 12 different cab companies and on every police car in all six precincts of Clark County.

Fourteen major hotels in the city distributed red ribbons to their guests, and Clark County designated a 21-mile stretch of road as the "first Red Ribbon Road in the state and in the nation."

The City of Las Vegas, Clark County and the

MADD Clark County chapter, proclaimed its first "red ribbon baby," born on December 10.

Sandy Heverly and Las Vegas Mayor, Ron Lurie, went up in a hot air balloon adorned with hundreds of red ribbons to symbolize how "MADD's spirits soar every time there is a reduction in alcohol-related fatalities."

Sky divers created a red bow in the sky with red smoke streaming from their feet.

Was it all just a show? Not by any means. During the duration of MADD's Project Red Ribbon campaign, Las Vegas had 39 straight days without a single alcohol-related fatality.

And just as important, it was the second year in a row (the city had done a large promotion the year before, too) that Las Vegas reported no drunk driving fatalities during the holiday season!

In Alabama, red ribbons were tied to memorial trees in local cemeteries in memory of victims killed in alcohol-related crashes.

In Oregon, the state's banking system distributed red ribbons through each of its teller windows and drive-throughs — handing out more than a million ribbons statewide.

In Georgia, the State Highway Patrol gave ribbons to every driver who applied for or renewed a driver's license during the holiday season.

And, in Kansas, the *Kansas City Star* inserted 350,000 red ribbons into newspapers delivered citywide.

Connie Sellecca
Actress Connie Sellecca has served the last four years as the national spokesperson for Project Red Ribbon.

"Drunk driving is a crime, and I am putting forth a special effort in spreading the anti-impaired driving message," she said. "I have an 8-year-old son, and I want him and others to have a future. It's critical that Americans take a stance and 'tie one on for safety.' "

But the greatest thing of all about this simple concept of tying a red ribbon on a door handle, or mirror, or antenna — is that it works!

That little red ribbon becomes a beacon, a warning beacon that reminds everyone who sees it — not just the driver of the car — about the dangers of drinking and driving.

And it works especially well because of the time of year.

It happens every day during the holidays. People, even with the best of intentions, get caught up in the festivities of a party and have too much to drink.

The alcohol they've had blurs their senses as earlier pledges not to drink and drive are about to be broken.

They get to their car and reach for the door handle. There's the red ribbon. Suddenly shining brightly, reminding them that the mistake they are about to make could be fatal!

That last minute reminder could save their life — and that of others out on the road that same night.

Saving lives. Like so many of MADD's programs, that's what Project Red Ribbon is all about.

Grief Knows No Bounds

There's never just one victim in a drunk driving crash. For every victim killed by a drunk, part of other people's lives are lost, too. Lost to the grief and sadness that can be so overwhelming.

Sometimes Death Begets Death

Sometimes the grief of losing a loved one to a drunk driver can be overpowering. Betty Stadler knows that. She started MADD in Idaho in 1988, a year after the death of her daughter, Carol. Betty's husband, Ben, died two years later. Never able to find a way to deal with his grief, he died of a broken heart.

Here's Betty's story:

Personal tragedy is my motivation for working with victims of drunk driving crashes. Our youngest daughter, Carol, was killed by a drunk driver when she was only 28. Carol was a wife, mother, daughter, sister and friend. Carol's husband, Kelley, age 31, suffered a broken neck in the same crash. The trauma of his injuries will be with him the rest of his life.

Our family received a memorial for Carol from a friend through MADD, Clakamas County, Oregon. We were also sent various pamphlets from MADD. The two which helped us the most were "Loss of a Child," and "Helping Children

Deal with Grief."

At times we really thought we were losing our minds. The grief was so intense and the hurt so very deep, we did not realize we were experiencing a natural part of the grieving process. After reading the pamphlets, we began to realize these feelings were "normal." We could also better relate to the actions of the little girls Carol left behind, Sarah, age 7, and Laura, age 4.

The knowledge and understanding gained from these materials were a great help to us in learning how to cope with our grief.

A friend who lost her son in a drunk driving crash six years ago has been a tremendous support to me. She seems to do the right thing at the right time, giving so much support. She truly understands what I feel.

Most important in working with victims is the knowledge I have gained by the unfortunate circumstance of being a victim. I know their pain first hand. A natural bond is formed by the common experience we share. Victim assistance is a top priority in my life.

I would like to share a poem I recently wrote:

WHAT IS IT?

It takes your soul and leaves it bare.
It takes your mind, you don't know where.
It takes your heart, as it breaks with pain.
It takes your body, you feel the strain.

Grief is the feeling I'm speaking of,
From the devastating loss of one you love.
It seems to come from the depths of hell,
I cry, "Dear Lord, will I ever be well?"

When a Mom dies

Most of us don't think about parents killed by drunk drivers. We think that since parents are expected to die before their children that it should not be so traumatic. That's not the case. To die in a drunk driving crash is not the dignified death we wish for our parents.

Kathy Hauze knows that all too well:

It all began on April 12, 1985. It was a beautiful spring day and a special day for me because I would be celebrating my 15th wedding anniversary and my sister's birthday. To my surprise, my mother dropped by our house that morning for a visit. She was on her way to a few yard sales and wanted me to go with her. Although I needed to do some paper work, I went with her anyway.

When we returned home, my mother said she was going to another yard sale in nearby Douglassville and asked me if I wanted to go. It was almost time for my son to get out of nursery school, so we talked about picking him up, getting some lunch, and then going to Douglassville. Mom could sense that I really didn't want to go, so she went alone.

At 11:20 a.m., that beautiful spring day, I watched my mother back her car out of my driveway, as she had done many times before, and drive away. The only thing different this time was that it would be the last time I would see her alive. In less than an hour she was dead.

On the way home from the yard sale, less than five miles from her house, a drunk driver killed her. One small consolation is that it happened so very fast, she did not suffer. However, in those few quick seconds, a drunk driver mangled, abused, and violated the most beautiful, loving woman in my life—just because he chose to mix drinking and driving.

My mother spent the final seconds of her life on a cold, black highway, defiled and made a public spectacle of by the curious crowd that had gathered around her. Such a cold, senseless ending to a wonderful lady's life nauseates me. The fact that my mother is dead hurts me enormously, but thinking about how she died makes me sick to my stomach.

I had always expected to be with mother when she died. Not only was I not with her, but no one was there when she died. As a result, I feel as if I don't have any part of her with me now.

The driving urge to go to her car kept bothering me, so the next morning I left my house alone and went to the junk yard. There, in the solitude, I went over her car with a fine-toothed comb, hoping beyond hope to find her or at least some small part of her. I saw, touched, smelled and even tasted the moment. Needless to say, I didn't find her. Although I never told anyone about going to Mom's car before now, I did what I felt that I needed to do for myself that day. I felt better as I left the junk yard because the gnawing feeling to

have Mom physically with me was finally gone.
As I pulled my car out of the drive, I finally knew
that mother would never be back with me again.

Today, I can close my eyes and easily picture
my Mother's blood in the car, but as the tears roll
down my cheeks, I thank God for helping me say
goodbye to my mother in the junk yard that day.
It was my first major step toward coping with her
violent, senseless death.

I became involved with MADD immediately
after my mother was killed. I was angry, as most
victims are, but I was also determined to find out
what would be done about her death. MADD was
the logical place to look for answers. I joined
MADD for purely selfish reasons. However, I
soon discovered I would stay for a selfless reason.
Now I want to try to prevent the same needless
tragedy from happening to someone else.

Working with MADD is a kind of therapy for
me. It helps me to feel better because I know
other people understand my pain, but it also
allows me an outlet for my desire to stop the
senseless crime of drunk driving.

I've walked in your shoes

Sometimes helping others helps make the grief a little
more palatable.

Marilyn Peffley has worked in MADD in Indiana
since 1983 and continues to be a gentle and loving advocate for others to whom she can say, "I know something of what you feel . . . for I've walked in your
shoes."

My first close experience with death came on

October 28, 1978 when my daughter, Delaine, who was 24 years old, was killed by a drunk driver. We were devastated. There is no way to compare the death of a child with the death of any other family member. From time to time you think about the fact that your spouse may die before you do. But not in your wildest dreams do you ever anticipate one of your children preceding you in death. It's not the natural order of things. Your children are meant to be here to look after you when you get old and unable to look after yourself.

One of the first and most difficult tasks I had to face was going to the home of Delaine's grand-parents and telling them the bad news. It was very disturbing to see the raw hurt and feel the anguish they experienced when the reality of what had happened to Delaine overtook them.

A friend of mine insisted that I take tranquil-izers to help me through the grieving process. I did not do that and I'm glad because I believe it would only have delayed the grieving process. I helped plan the memorial service that we held for Delaine. Throughout this time it appeared to many that I was very strong, while others were grieving. It was not that I was not experiencing sorrow. It was that the shroud of grief was within me, cushioning me and protecting me from the reality of what had occurred. Who can tell when the shock wears off and you drift into another stage of grief?

When people came to visit at the funeral home, I stayed in control. It was I who comforted those who had come to comfort us. Long lines of people came to us in our time of sorrow, waiting to greet us and to give us a hug. A large number of people attended Delaine's memorial service.

Strange things happen to your system throughout the grief process that you don't always understand. There is still no such thing as a normal day. When everyone else returns to their routines, your whole life continues to lay in shreds. The pieces can't fit together any more because some of the pieces are no longer there.

After Delaine's death came the realization that nothing would ever be the same again. Not ever! I simply tried to keep afloat in the sea of life. I remember that when I went out in public, nothing seemed any different. No one had noticed the change that I had experienced or saw the hurt I felt. I found myself wanting to scream out, "How can you act so normal? Don't you know my daughter is dead?"

I wrestled with how to describe the structure of my family as I talked to strangers. I was determined not to ignore Delaine, yet when I mentioned what happened, the conversation was suddenly over. People just didn't know what to say or how to react when they learned that a drunk driver killed my daughter.

Card stores are very painful places for me to visit because all those lovely "daughter" cards leap out at me. I still feel angry every time I buy her flowers. It seems I should be buying her a gift instead of flowers for her grave.

The man who killed Delaine served 44 days in

jail. There was no MADD organization in 1978 to turn to for help. How could the reckless behavior of one person be treated so lightly? I became infuriated with a judicial system that treated drunk driving as simply "accidental." I decided if anything was ever going to change, victims like myself would be the ones to do it.

Working with victims has been natural for me as I work in MADD. When people learn that I have had a tragedy in my own family, they tend to trust me with their pain. The motivation to keep me going is knowing first hand the pain they are experiencing. If there is any way I can ease that pain, just a tiny bit, then I want to do it.

I honestly believe that nothing is ever so bad that something good can't come from it. Perhaps it is from my own experiences of knowing a hurt beyond measure that I am able to identify with another victim's pain. This certainly is not something I would have ever chosen to do. But since I'm in this position, maybe there is something that I can do or say that might make the victim's load a little easier.

Community in Crisis: The Kentucky School Bus Crash

The nation reacted in horror to the worst drunk driving crash in our history near Carrollton, Kentucky on May 14, 1988.

Larry Mahoney ran into a school bus owned by the Radcliff Assembly of God Church as it was returning home from a youth outing to Kings Island Amusement Park in Cincinnati.

According to investigating officials, Mahoney was driving the wrong way with a blood alcohol count of .24 on a Kentucky interstate highway.

A total of 27 people, 24 of them youth, were killed in the crash.

Fourteen others were seriously injured and hundreds more were emotionally scarred as a result of this tragedy.

Janie Fair's daughter, Shannon, was killed in that tragedy. Janie is now president of the MADD chapter in Hardin County, Kentucky:

> It's your worst dream come true. Twenty seven of your loved ones, friends and neighbors are massacred in a drunk driving collision. The driver of the small pick up was headed the wrong way on the interstate and the results lead to a fiery collision that brought death, pain and suffering. My daughter, Shannon, was on that church bus loaded with youth and sponsors as they headed home

that night from a church outing. Their day of fun turned into a nightmare beyond comprehension for us all.

The driver of the truck was described by his friends as a "good old boy." He was directly responsible for the deaths of twenty seven people that night and was found to have a blood alcohol content of .24 percent. That's more than twice the legal limit of .10 percent for driving while intoxicated in Kentucky.

May 14, 1988 was a fateful day, one that none of the community will ever forget. Shannon was an eighth grade student and an honor student at Radcliff Middle School. She had participated in classes designed for gifted/talented students. She was a teenager like most teenagers and had many friends. Some of her friends died with her that night.

Shannon had been baptized the Easter Sunday morning before she was killed and was a member of Stithton Baptist Church.

There is a great deal to be said about what happened to our beautiful Shannon and her friends that fateful day, but sometimes it's hard to put feelings into words and frustrations onto paper. Sometimes the hurt is too fresh to be verbalized and we have to wait for time to heal before we can speak what our heart feels.

Pause with me a few moments and think about Shannon. She was a bright attractive, kind, loving young lady who should have had a full life ahead of her. She was only fourteen and everybody knows how much fun life is at fourteen, or is supposed to be.

Shannon was a joy to us parents. She kept things exciting around the house as she talked about all the things that were happening with her friends and school. She was almost always busy doing one thing or another and since it was nearly summer time, her thoughts were turning to summer vacation. Laughter and happiness filled the air wherever our Shannon was around.

But now the laughter has grown silent. There is no more giggling down the hallways or phone calls from friends who want to go somewhere. Now stillness and quiet sadness has replaced the laughter that filled the house, and the entire family hurts deeply inside. Once happy faces now display the torment that spills from the heart, drains the soul, and makes us look stressed and strained.

Shannon's brother will never be the same again, either. His sister is gone. Never again, this side of heaven, can he look into her lovely face and tease her, joke with her, have fun with her. Never again can they sit at the dinner table and talk about all the things that were familiar to them. Never again will he know the pleasure of spending time with his sister. Don is a surviving sibling now and he is learning how very difficult that can be.

The family has a lot of time to think about what might have been. We have a lot of time to remember. We have joys that are ours to share concerning Shannon and we have memories to talk about of our life with Shannon because, you see, Shannon will always be part of our lives.

The Carroll County jury that found the drunk driver guilty on 81 of 82 charges did sentence him to jail time. He was found guilty of second-degree manslaughter, first-degree assault, first- and second-degree wanton endangerment, and driving under the influence.

While the nationwide hue and cry for tougher drunk driving laws that followed the Kentucky school bus tragedy was welcomed, it was too late for those like Shannon Fair who were killed as a result of Larry Mahoney's decision to drink and drive.

The immediate need was support for the families, loved ones, friends and neighbors of those victims.

At the request of Kentucky's Attorney General, MADD and the National Organization for Victim Assistance (NOVA) responded to the bus crash tragedy by immediately sending a crisis team into the community to provide training for local support service groups. Intensive training was provided to mental health counselors, clergy, teachers, community leaders and others to help them better understand the needs of the victim families.

Janice Lord, MADD's director of victim services, and her husband, Dr. Richard Lord, a minister, were included on the team and continue to this day an ongoing relationship with the Radcliff community.

The goals of the Community Crisis Response Team were:

(1) To assist local leaders and caregivers in planning their immediate and long-term response to the crisis;

(2) To provide training, support and recognition to the caregivers, and;

(3) To assist the caregivers by offering them model

"debriefings" in which they might ventilate their own reactions to the trauma as well as learn the components of a meaningful debriefing.

The first evening, caregivers such as police, funeral home directors, school counselors and others listed above, gathered to meet each other and share what they were doing or planned to do to help. They committed to attend the following day's training and helped identify others who would benefit from the training.

The next morning the team provided training on short-term crisis reaction, long-term crisis response, children in crisis, and how to conduct debriefings.

The remainder of the weekend was spent with team members going in pairs to conduct debriefings. Sites included the school which most of the dead and injured children had attended, a hospital which had been the employment place of a nurse and her two children who were killed, another hospital where many of the seriously injured had been admitted, a meeting of community clergy who were struggling with their own responses to God in the aftermath of the tragedy, and the church where a majority of the victims were members.

An unusual press conference followed, in which members of the press were invited not only to learn about the role of the team but to ventilate their own anguish over trying to be responsible journalists in the midst of deep sympathy and outrage about what had happened.

Shortly after the team's departure, key caregivers in the community developed their own Crisis Response Team to continue coordination of services as well as to offer support to victims and other professionals. Both MADD and NOVA continued phone and letter consultation to the team.

Victims reach out to victims

In early July, the local Hardin County MADD chapter and several victim families invited MADD's National Office to bring together a second team of victims of drunk driving crashes. Team members could offer personal support and hope to the victim families, most of whom were now coming out of shock and beginning to experience incredible emotional pain in the aftermath of the crash. The team was developed and spent the weekend of July 29-31 in the Radcliff community, offering support to approximately 50 victims.

MADD Victim Team members included both the bereaved and the injured.

Dorothy Mercer from Richmond, Kentucky, is a psychologist who suffered permanent injury in a drunk driving crash in Michigan in 1981. In addition to her expertise on injury, she addressed the family dynamics which can change as a result of trauma.

Sharon Sikora, from Phoenix, Arizona, was rear-ended by a drunk driver in 1981, causing her car to burst into flames that burned her over 95 percent of her body. She could provide first hand understanding of the recovery process from severe burns.

Betty Jane Spencer, MADD State Administrator from Florida, was the only team member who had not been involved in a drunk driving crash. However, the murder of her four sons and her own injury in 1976 gave her a victim's understanding of what it means to suffer multiple losses and respond to community crisis. She was particularly valuable in reaching out to the younger siblings of those killed or injured.

Millie Webb of Franklin, Tennessee, suffered a drunk driving crash in 1971 in which she and her husband were severely burned and her 4-year-old daughter and 19-month-old nephew were killed. Sharing her recovery pilgrimage, both as a bereaved parent and a burn victim, made her an extremely valuable asset to the team.

Friday evening brought together everyone in the Radcliff community who was interested. And the Colvin Community Center was filled for the meeting in which MADD leaders, including local president Lelia Haddle presented local and state goals. The team was introduced and Betty Jane Spencer shared suggestions for the community's response to the victims.

All of Saturday was devoted to confidential support of the victim families (no press allowed). Each team member shared his or her remembrance of where they were ten weeks after their tragedy and offered helpful information about "what they know now that they wish they had known then."

Later the families were divided into the bereaved and the injured, and their families and friends, to meet informally with designated team members. Later, the victims were divided into men, women, adolescents and children to talk about problems unique to their sex or age.

On Sunday, the team attended Radcliff Assembly of God Church and met with other victims before departing for home in the late afternoon.

While members of both the MADD/NOVA Crisis Response Team and the MADD Victim Team recall many poignant memories from their interventions, many center on the seemingly "forgotten victims" —

—the funeral director and his staff who had to face 27 charred bodies at one time;

—the clergy who were forced to struggle with the concept of a living God who allows tragedy, all the while offering support and encouragement to the community;

—the school teachers who had come to love the children in their classrooms during the preceding nine months, but who now had to face, with no training in crisis reaction, classroom after classroom with three, four, five empty seats;

—the "girlfriends and boyfriends" of those who were killed and who were not afforded the right to a place among the mourning;

—the injured who were consistently told they should feel lucky to be alive in the midst of painful physical recovery, deep grief, guilt for being alive, and uncontrollable nightmares and flashbacks;

—and the brothers and sisters of those killed who escaped the bus and then felt guilty for not being able to save their siblings.

Janice Lord expressed appreciation for the many MADD members who had expressed a willingness to participate in the team. Even though not all could be included, those who did participate were aware of the prayers and support of the many caring and compassionate victims and concerned citizens of MADD throughout the country.

Later, Wayne Cox, a 14-year-old survivor of the school bus crash described the emotional scars that will remain with him throughout his life.

What happened to me and the 39 other survivors of the Kentucky school bus crash last May

14, I wouldn't wish upon my most hated enemy
or even the man who caused that day to be dis-
astrous by driving drunk.

That day was one of the most influential in my
life.

To share with you my views on drunk driving, I
would have to share with you my experiences
since that night.

It was that night I lost my childhood sense of
invincibility. It was turned into a more mature
sense of reality and a less juvenile knowledge of
the world and its dangers, in this case . . . drunk
driving.

On that day, 40 people's lives were changed so
they would never see life the same again. More
sadly, 27 people would never more experience
life.

Are 27 people's lives worth being lost for one
man's ignorance and irresponsibility?

The effects of drunk driving don't just end with
death. Consider those who survived but still suffer physically every day in a hospital room. Consider those who survived but still suffer mentally
every day in a world that slows for no one.

The lucky ones are those who lived . . . or are
they? Perhaps the lucky ones are those who died
because they are now in a place much more glorious than this.

But . . . does luck enter into it?

During this year, I have seen many things; the
other survivors, with the constant reminder of
that day as they are forced to look at their dis-
figured bodies; families grieving over the death of

a loved one. These are things I shouldn't have had to see.

My friends and I carried two of our best friends' bodies to their graves . . . something we shouldn't have had to do.

I have felt grief, confusion, hatred . . . feelings that I shouldn't have had to feel.

Yet, I experienced a strong bond of love holding our community together. I could talk to God and find peace and comfort in Him.

Along with 40 other survivors, I've learned many things. None of this would have had to be faced if it weren't for one man's very poor choice.

What happened on May 14th can't be changed . . . nor can it be forgotten.

On May 14, 1989, an emotional memorial service was held to observe the first anniversary of the Kentucky tragedy.

With emotions heightened by the fact that the anniversary fell on Mother's Day, thousands of friends and family members gathered to take part in the community-wide event.

The services began with a monument dedication and unveiling ceremony for the memorial entitled "Our Precious Loss." The granite memorial consists of two dark granite slabs, one containing the names of those who were killed in the crash and the other bearing the names of those who survived.

Kentucky's Secretary of Transportation, Milo Bryant was the speaker for the dedication service which also included special prayers and songs.

Afterward, an appreciation service was held, with MADD receiving an appreciation certificate for its work with those victimized by the crash. In all, some 140 organizations, individuals and businesses were recognized for helping pull the pieces together after the crash.

The ceremonies concluded with a memorial service highlighted by the attendance of Kentucky Governor Wallace Wilkinson who expressed his strong support in the battle to stop drunk driving.

A letter was read from President and Mrs. Bush, extending their sympathy and offering their own commitment in the fight to end drunk driving.

The memorial services brought together the local community and the national media with a potent reminder about the pain and suffering caused by such a senseless tragedy.

Living Victims

Despite the fact that more than 23,000 Americans are killed each and every year by drunk drivers, that number pales when compared to the number of injuries attributable to drunk driving—more than 500,000 each and every year.

Every minute, someone else is injured in a drunk driving crash.

And, while some people claim that those who survive such crashes are the lucky ones, most of those victims might have difficulty describing themselves as lucky.

Living with the Pain

Ricardo Melendez is Vice President of MADD, Ventura County, California and also works as Hispanic Outreach Coordinator and Victim Advocate. He writes from the perspective of an injured victim:

Someone a long time ago anonymously wrote some thoughts down that help me get through some of the tough times:

"If any life of mine may ease the burden of another,

God give me love and care and Strength,

To help my ailing brother."

The only thing I would add to this writing of long ago would be, "as well as my ailing sister." There are so many who need love and care and I believe that because of what I have experienced, I can identify with those who have special needs.

On April 6, 1988, I became one of the thousands of Americans who are seriously injured by drunk drivers. Never had I thought I would become one of that number who survive a collision with a drunk driver and live with serious injuries for the rest of my life.

Since the crash I've been involved in a difficult transition period in my life. It has taken considerable time to get used to the inconveniences I have to deal with, including the loss of my right leg above the knee.

I believe learning to live with what has happened to me has aided me in understanding how to help others through their trials.

In my work with MADD, I've been able to establish a good relationship with local law enforcement agencies, District Attorneys Office, Victim/Witness Unit, and other agencies and organizations that can be utilized by a victim and/or their families after a crash.

Recovery and acceptance of life-altering injuries is not easy. Each recovering victim must realize that it takes a great deal of time to adjust to a new and different lifestyle. You have to change the way you do things.

With all the activities and labels I carry around, I thank God that I am allowed to continue to wear the label, "Daddy." The time my little girl and I spend together is precious to me. And, giving credit where credit is due, she is the big reason that I have come so far after such a traumatic occurrence. She is the light of her "Daddy's" life.

23 Years of Surgery

Marti Page, State Administrator of MADD, Illinois, knows better than most people what it's like to battle injuries inflicted by a drunk driver. This is her story:

Excited, very pretty in her new party dress, and just a little bit anxious, 15-year-old Marti Mull gazed out the windshield as her father drove her to the dance. Her mind drifted from visions of the boy she hoped would come, to a prayer that no one else would have a dress like hers, and back to her delight that her dear daddy thought she was the most beautiful girl in the world. The year was 1964.

The next thing she remembers is waking up in a hospital and staring at her left leg hanging in traction with a metal rod sticking out of both sides of it. She could not speak because of the tracheotomy tube in her throat. As her fingers traced her throat and then her face, she was horrified to feel the gaudy stitches binding together deep lacerations around her neck, on her face, and in her head. As the pain ebbed and then finally diminished, she knew she would never be beautiful again.

As she questioned her mother, she learned that she had nearly died while pinned beneath the dashboard of the car, awaiting her rescue. She and her dad had been hit head on and she had been thrown through the windshield, her throat slit as she came back through the broken glass. She had been in a coma five days and her condition was critical.

Her daddy, Gus Mull, had also suffered serious injury, but more than that, he felt the aching heaviness of a broken heart because of what had happened to his lit-

tle girl. Like all parents, he agonized over being unable
to protect the child he loved so much. He died a few
years later.

The 21-year-old driver responsible for the crash had
crossed the center lane slamming head on into Marti
and her dad's car. His only sanction was suspension of
his driver's license for 90 days. Since he was uninsured,
Marti's family was responsible for all her medical care.
Surgeries continued for the next 23 years—the most recent in 1987.

But the fighting spirit which kept Marti alive during
the first two and a half months in the hospital and during countless painful surgeries works well for her today.
She graduated from the University of Iowa in 1970 and
worked several years in estate and financial planning.
She became a volunteer for MADD as treasurer of the
newly-formed Chicagoland chapter in 1985. In January, 1987, MADD-Illinois was organized at the state
level with Marti as State Administrator.

MADD, Illinois has encouraged the Illinois legislature to pass some of the toughest drunk driving laws in
the country. The state now has 15 chapters.

One must look closely now to see the scars, and actually, very few people notice them. Marti has survived
her tragedy to become an assertive young woman determined to right at least one wrong in America today—
drunk driving. Her eyes shine, her teeth sparkle, and
her heart glows with love of life. Her daddy would have
been very, very proud of what his little girl has become.

"Don't Call Me Lucky!"

MADD has a special brochure called "Don't Call Me
Lucky!" It is intended for those injured in drunk driv-

ing crashes and their family and friends.

One section of the pamphlet offers the following suggestions for friends and families of injured victims:

Learning about the crash, rushing to the hospital, and seeing your loved one in pain, pale, bloody, and lifeless is a trauma all its own. You probably experienced shock, anxiety, and terrible dread. Even though your focus is primarily on your injured loved one, understand that you, too, are traumatized. Seek help and support you need in order to cope.

*Always remember that it could just as easily have been you who was injured . . .

*Recovery of your loved one will rarely be complete . . .

*Try to be a nurturer rather than a caretaker . . .

*Work toward normalizing the victim's experience, not minimizing it . . .

*Learn to be comfortable with rage and despair and encourage expression of them . . .

*Expect guilt, especially if someone else was killed in the crash . . .

*Expect anniversary reactions . . .

*Allow the victim to tell and re-tell the story of what happened . . .

*Help the victim label his or her feelings . . .

*Understand that it is normal for the victim to move forward, then fall back . . .

*Help the victim process nightmares, flashbacks, and night terrors . . .

*Help the victim talk about second victimizations . . .

 *Give honest, reasonable recognition at signs of recovery . . .

 *Encourage the victim to socialize, but don't insist on it . . .

 *Seeing the one you love suffer so much can break your heart. Take care of yourself . . .

The pamphlet also includes a poem written by Dorothy Mercer, a psychologist who was seriously injured in a drunk driving crash:

I live with my injuries.
People say to me, "Aren't you lucky!"
And they don't understand
Why my face suddenly freezes
And my voice becomes tense.

I can say I'm lucky
If I so choose on any given day.
But when others say it,
I feel as if
They discount my pain
And don't recognize my costs,
Counting me only as alive or dead
No matter how hard it may be
To endure living.

Some days I am glad:
Life itself is all that matters,
And I savor it.

But when I hurt too much,
Or am told I won't fully heal,
When I can not work or play as before,

Or feel I'm a burden on others,
Then I don't feel lucky at all!
I feel cheated!

Some days I even wish
I had died rather than live like this.
So please don't tell me
That I'm lucky
to only be injured.

Tell me instead
That you're glad I'm still here,
And let me know why.
Tell me that you care about
My grief, pain, anger and adjustments.
Tell me you'll willingly rehear
My disappointments, loss and frustrations.
And have patience while I relearn to live.

Then someday I can tell you
How lucky I am—to have someone
Who understands and accepts my sorrows
And who also shares my joys!

Engulfed in Flames

Sharon Sikora, Arizona State Coordinating Chairperson and MADD National Vice President for Victim Issues, knows what it is like to be a severely injured victim of a drunk driving crash.

I'M ON TOP OF THE WORLD! I knew those words were meant for me. WHY? I lived in glorious Phoenix, Arizona—young, attractive, with a beautiful daughter and a wonderful career, not to mention a fantastic social life. Does it sound like every woman's dream? It was for me.

You may ask, "Who is this person?" I am not a noted celebrity, movie star, politician or rich person. I am an average American citizen—just like you.

Just back from a vacation with friends in Mackinac Island, Michigan, tan and rested, I was all set to begin another whirlwind fall-winter. August 26, 1981 is a day I will always remember and wish I could forget. But forget I cannot. Looking every day at scars from head to toe won't let me.

On that warm August evening, on my way to a seminar, I was rear-ended by a drunk driver. In just a few minutes, my entire life was changed. My car exploded and I was trapped in that burning inferno, on fire myself! There was no way out. The windows were up, and within seconds the plastic had melted, leaving no handles to open the doors. The car was so engulfed in flames no one could get near it. I prayed to God to help me get out or take me fast. Then the windows blew out and I found myself diving out on the hot pavement and rolling. That was the last thing I remember until much later when I woke up in the emergency room of a hospital.

Weeks passed before I learned that a man watering his lawn had seen the car on fire and me struggling to get out. He turned his hose on the windows, which made them blow out. God had answered my prayers—I knew it.

Those first days there was doubt that I would

live. The rest is a nightmare of days, weeks and months of struggle against the odds. Would I ever see, walk, talk, or hear again?

I was burned over 95 percent of my body. Sixty five percent had second and third degree burns. The skin that wasn't burned was removed to cover parts that were. I was in and out of consciousness for three weeks before I realized what had happened to me. In that three week period I feel that God gave me a choice to live or to die. I chose to face the incredible pain and forge ahead with God's help.

PAIN—always that incredible pain! Again, God gave me a choice to be relieved of all the pain. You know what my choice was since I am here writing about it. I have since learned that those two choices came to me while I died on the operating table! No one can tell me God isn't there when you need Him. I am living proof that He is.

The road ahead of me was to be a very long one. After a month in critical condition intensive care isolation, the doctors said I had a fifty-fifty chance. No one knew if I would ever function again as a normal human being.

I spent another month in isolation. Because of the seriousness of my condition, I was limited to five visitors. Only two could come into the room at a time for a short time. My going in and out of consciousness cut it even shorter. The loneliness was almost as bad as the excruciating pain. The worst part was not seeing a face. People came in covered with masks, gowns, paper hats, paper shoes and rubber gloves. Everyone had to dress this way. Was this a nightmare or a movie? No; it was all too real.

Before I went home, I asked for a mirror. No one prepared me for what I saw. Who was that monster looking out at me? What a shock! Was the struggle really worth it all? That haunting question seemed always there. I prayed, "Dear God please help me handle all this!" All those things I took for granted like brushing my teeth and washing my hair had to be learned all over again. I had therapy every day for the next six months to learn to move, to walk, and to use my arms and hands. The physical pain was excruciating. Would it never end? I called therapy my torture chamber but I knew it was necessary if I ever wanted to function normally again.

After months of grueling therapy the plastic surgeries began. The first was to release my right arm from my chest. They had melted together in the fire! At the same time, they operated on the right hand to straighten melted-bent fingers. I prayed it would be successful. I wanted more than anything to be able to dress myself again.

After all the open wounds had healed, I had to be fitted for special garments to flatten out the burned scar tissue. I was fitted from head to toe and looked the part of a strange being from another planet. Now I had to deal with stares wherever I went. They didn't understand. I had a new kind of pain to deal with. Emotional pain. I truly believe the emotional pain is worse than the physical pain. To help ease the emotional pain, I became involved in a burn support group at the hospital and with MADD. Several people in both these groups became my friends and helped with a large part of my recovery. To them and my family, I owe so much more than I can ever repay. I ask God to bless them every day.

Several years have now passed since that day in August 1981. I have had numerous operations to remove scar tissue, make new lips, graft and sand my face, to mention a few. Over 80 plastic reconstructive surgeries have been performed on me. Total expense exceeded $250,000.

What happened to the drunk driver? Nothing for over a year—nothing. Then finally a court date and sentencing. The judge gave the drunk driver five years probation, 600 hours of community service (which he never served) and an order to repay the medical bills not covered to date by MY insurance (which he tried to get out of numerous times). It doesn't seem like much for completely altering the life of another human being.

And, my story is not over. It may never really end. Every day when I look in the mirror, I am reminded of what happened. However, I know that if it had not been for MADD and my burn support group, Ashes to Life, I would not be in such good psychological shape today. I also know that my faith in God, all the prayers from friends, family and even strangers helped me make it through. I am happy to be alive, living in Arizona and committed to making our community a safer place to live.

Anyone out there reading this—don't think
something like this can't happen to you, your
family or someone you love. IT CAN. It's all too
real—believe me!

"The glue that holds my heart together."

Millie Webb also knows what it's like to battle the
physical pain of recovering from burn wounds while
trying to cope with the devastating emotional pain of
losing a little daughter. This is her story:

Millie thanked God every day for the beauty of her
life. She and Roy had a wonderful marriage, a beautiful
4-year-old daughter, Lori, and she was nearly eight
months pregnant.

Returning home from Nashville with their 19-month-
old nephew, Mitchell, about 10 p.m. on a hot August
night, their car was rear ended by an intoxicated juvenile driving 110 miles per hour.

Millie's father, Robert Irvin, was one of the fireman
called to extinguish the fiery crash. Because the car was
burned beyond recognition, he did not learn until returning to the fire station that the victims were his own
family.

Little Mitchell, with burns over 90 percent of his
body, died the next morning. Beautiful little Lori died
two weeks later from the burns that covered over 75
percent of her body. Roy suffered burns over 42 percent of his body and required pins in his hands from the
damage done trying to fight the flames. He was hospit-
alized for two months.

Millie was thrown from the car, but still suffered
burns over 75 percent of her body and was in intensive
care for three months.

Neither Roy nor Millie knew that Lori had been killed until long after she had been buried.

Since Millie was not expected to live, the doctors decided to try and deliver her baby although they had virtually no hope that the child would be born alive.

But three days after the crash, a healthy baby girl, Kara, was born.

It was months before Millie could hold, or even touch, her infant because her skin was so badly burned. Relatives cared for Kara until Millie could tolerate a foreign body touching her raw skin.

Then, as if this family needed more pain, when Kara was several months old, the family began to notice she had difficulty focusing her eyes. When she was nine months old, an ophthalmologist gave Millie and Roy the heartbreaking news. Kara was legally blind.

Today, Millie looks back over those months and years with deep gratitude for the constant support of family, friends, doctors and nurses, all who became victims of the ordeal. But she credits God and her husband Roy with her emotional recovery. "I am convinced God knew I would need someone strong like Roy to lean on. Most people consider what happened to us a tragedy. I tell people, all of our heartaches were a result of that one night of terror, but the rest of our lives have been blessed."

Millie has had 12 surgeries since the crash and needs more, but is raising Kara and fighting for her daughter's rights as a visually-impaired child. She and Roy had another child, Ashlea, which they consider a blessing from God.

The young offender was sentenced to two years probation for the crime he committed. The juvenile judge pointed out that a juvenile court is to rehabilitate, not punish. The driver has received at least two more DWI's since the Webb crash with blood alcohol far above the legal limit.

Millie's work with victims of drunk drivers has included the families and victims of the Kentucky school bus tragedy.

Says she, "The story of each victim who shares his or her pain with me entwines around my heart. Little do they realize that as I am able to support them, they, in turn, continue to support me. As I still deal with my own family's victimization on a daily basis, their stories are the glue that holds my heart together and gives me the strength to go on. I can never thank MADD enough for the difference it's made in my life. If even one family can be spared what we have endured, it's worth it all.

Sharon Sikora and Millie Webb were both members of the MADD crisis team that went to Radcliff, Kentucky to lend assistance and psychological support to victims of the school bus crash there. Many of those victims were severely burned. Sharon's and Millie's presence and willingness to discuss their conditions from first-hand perspective, gave many of them the inspiration to aggressively pursue their recovery.

"Other" Victims

Following a drunk driving crash, MADD's initial focus is on the immediate victims, those whose injury or death has been caused by the drunk driver.

Next comes attention to the families, loved ones and friends of those victims, to help them cope with the loss, the grief and, all too often the struggle with our system of justice.

But in almost every drunk driving crash, there's still another group of victims, a group whose role as heroes often overshadows their role as victims, but who suffer deeply from the consequences of drunk driving nonetheless.

They're the emergency personnel, police, firemen, rescue squad members, ambulance drivers, paramedics, physicians, emergency room attendants and more who, despite their incredible professionalism, never become hardened to the horrors they face.

What follows is from an article in Volume 2, Number 1, of *MADDvocate*, a magazine published by MADD for victims and their advocates.

A neurological surgeon from Texarkana, Dr. George L. Bohmfalk, sent the following note to MADD along with a contribution:

Last night I saw the serious dedication and passion of one of MADD's volunteers on a very well done piece about drunk driving on the television

program *48 Hours*. I felt great pride for having
donated to MADD in the past and resolved to
send more shortly.

Within an hour, I was called to the emergency
room to see a young man who had been run over
by the recognized "town drunk." His injuries
were fatal.

Later on that same evening, I returned to the
hospital to treat a five-month-old boy who was
severely injured when his car was struck from behind by an intoxicated driver. That baby will
probably be retarded and physically impaired as a
result.

Paramedic Shares in the Grief . . . and Anger
Paramedics called to the scene of a crash pray they
will be able to remember all their training when they
would rather be screaming or crying. One paramedic,
Sandra Stamper, shared her unforgettable experience.

Arriving on the scene, I was awed at the tangl-
ed mass of metal and glass in the roadway. Being
the first on the scene, the serenity of the night did
nothing to assuage my fear of the unknown.

My partner and I grabbed our equipment and
ran as we became aware of the moans, groans,
screaming, and cursing of the victims. With only
slight relief, we heard the oncoming EMS Unit
and Fire Department.

It was so dark . . . but in a few moments a
police officer pulled his car alongside the wrecked
mass so he could shine his light inside.

There, lying halfway out of the shattered windshield, covered with blood and her right arm

nearly severed, was the woman who had been screaming. She was still trying to scream, but her voice was becoming weaker with each gasping breath. Another paramedic took over her care and I rushed to the other victim, a male.

His eyes were staring at something I couldn't see. No pulse. No breathing. Nothing. But to be very sure, I knew I had to put the EKG leads on him. I opened his shirt and saw that part of the dashboard had broken off and pierced his heart like an arrow. As I placed a sheet over him, I heard someone ask if I had taken care of the child.

"What child?" A police officer and I began to search. Someone else found the baby in a ditch. She was breathing but had a bluish bump on her forehead and crown. She was unconscious. Severe head trauma was likely, so we had to move quickly. We placed her carefully on a backboard, using sandbags on either side of her head to keep her still. As she was loaded into our vehicle, her mother was loaded into another ambulance to be transported to the hospital.

I hung my head and wanted to cry, but I had my little patient to care for. As I entered the vehicle, my partner joined me to tell about his patient, the driver.

As he shared his assessment with me, his voice gave his bitterness away. His patient sustained only minor injuries, mostly small lacerations and abrasions. His patient was furious because his bottle of whiskey was broken. His patient had stated, "I paid five dollars for that bottle and I'm going to sue that other guy for it."

Doctors Bear a Burden

Then there is the dreadful experience of the physician who must face a room full of anxious and frightened family members and tell them that their loved ones will not be coming home . . . ever again. It is not easy to be called from one's bed at night and then go to work the next day with no sleep, and function professionally.

Why do they do it? Dr. David Kleinberg, a family physician from Milwaukee, says that when he came home from Vietnam, he was treated with disdain by people who were angry about something over which they had no control. "But," he says, "Vietnam in no way compares to the tragedy that I, as a physician, see coming from the streets of America."

Kleinberg goes on, "Doctors have children just like the rest of you. I would like to tell you we go home from work after seeing this kind of thing and sleep, but we frequently can't because it makes us sick in our hearts. Drunk driving is a preventable problem, and no one is more committed to eliminating it than the physician."

MADD salutes the medical profession, with respect and gratitude. We join you in an ever-increasing commitment to stop the violence . . . for everybody's sake.

Out of a scientific consensus that alcohol causes deterioration of driving skills at .05% BAC or even lower, the American Medical Association makes the following recommendations:

1. Public education urging drivers not to drink;

2. Adoption by all states of .05% BAC *per se* evidence of alcohol-impaired driving.*

3. Legal drinking age of 21 in all states (now accomplished);

4. Adoption by all states of administrative driver's license suspension in drunk driving cases;

5. Encouragement of the automobile industry to develop a safety module that thwarts operation of vehicles by an intoxicated individual.

Journal of the American Medical Association, 1986 (255:527)

And the police are no more immune to the suffering they see than are the medical personnel, as evidenced by this letter written by a police sergeant to the parents of Cheryl Regenauer a year and a half after her death, at the conclusion of the criminal trial.

Dear Mr. & Mrs. Regenauer,

Even as I write this letter, I see your daughter's face. I did not know Cheryl or get to know her. Yet I have seen her face a hundred times since the early morning hours of July 3. The visions of that night will never fade away.

July 3, 1986, was like thousands of other nights for me. I was assigned a patrol squad on the Southside. The night had been uneventful but busy. My tour of duty (7:00 PM to 3:00 AM) was winding to a close, and I was looking forward to the coming holiday.

---

*(MADD opposes driving impaired by any measurable alcohol but advocates .08 BAC as an achievable goal for the *per se* limit.)

Just before midnight, I stopped to buy a soda and took a call to investigate a personal injury crash. An ambulance had been sent. Several minutes later, the radio cracked again "Squad 596, be advised second call—fire department and paramedics enroute."

The crash scene was several blocks from my own home, and I worried that the crash might involve a neighbor, friend, or loved one. I tried to prepare myself mentally for the worst that could happen.

I arrived a few minutes later. The fire department and several other squad cars were already on the scene. As I stepped from my squad car, I was relieved that the two vehicles were unfamiliar and didn't appear to be extensively damaged. But as I hurried across the intersection, I saw a body lying on the pavement. The silence was deafening.

The paramedics did not have to tell me that there was nothing they could do. I could see it in their faces—their grief etched in their furrowed brows, the sadness in their hushed voices.

I knelt down to examine Cheryl's injuries and looked into her face. She was, despite her injuries, a beautiful young woman—a woman who had everything to live for. Looking at Cheryl, I thought about my own daughter. Could this happen to her? Would she spend nineteen years on this earth, loving and being loved, only to be taken in an instant by the criminal negligence of a drunken stranger? You will never know the sadness that I felt. Ten years of training and experience did not prepare me for the horrors of that morning.

So it was again painful for me to read the article about the trial in this morning's paper. All of the memories of that sad night came back again.

I was especially angered to read the offender's father's claim that his son was "just plain irresponsible" and that the driver of Cheryl's car was partly responsible for the crash.

The fact is, the offender was intoxicated that night—so intoxicated that he could not tell me which direction he was driving. He just stood there and said, "Look at my father's new van."

Cheryl's girlfriend, on the other hand, appeared completely sober. I did not smell any alcohol on her breath, her speech was normal, and—aside from her injuries—she appeared perfectly normal. She was able to give me an account of the crash and her actions. It appears to me that the offender and his family, even now, cannot escape the responsibility for this crash and are still trying to escape the consequences of their actions.

I cannot hope to know the anguish and grief that you have suffered since your daughter's death. It was a tragic loss.

She did, however, not die completely in vain. She is still speaking to me—her voice speaking out, sending a clear message to all those who would drink and drive. Her face is forever in my memory.

MADD encourages officers who investigate crashes to allow their humanness to show when they deliver death notifications and later on as they interact with victim families. Because the officer was often the last person to see the victim alive, he or she has knowledge about "the last moments" which mean a great deal to the family. The above letter, a true act of compassion and honesty, was very meaningful for Cheryl's family.

Repeat Offenders = More Victims

Try to explain to the victim of a drunk driver why it happened. It's very, very difficult.

Try to explain to that same victim why the person who did this to them got off with such a lenient sentence. It's almost impossible.

But worst of all, try to explain to that victim why the drunk was even on the road after prior convictions! There is no explanation!

When repeat drunk driving offenders are allowed back on the streets, tragedy reoccurs.

The Father's Day "Present"

MADD receives letters every day from families who have been victims of drunk drivers. Many letters contain contributions to help MADD continue its efforts to end the tragedy of drunk driving.

But rarely, if ever, has a letter had the impact of one we received from the family of Richard Welch, a 44-year-old husband and father of two daughters. The letter itself was powerful, but it also contained a $50 bill. With stains on it.

Richard was killed by a drunk driver on Father's Day 1987, two hours before a planned family cookout.

His daughters had given him the $50 bill that morning as a Father's Day present, so he could buy some equipment for his new hobby, scuba diving.

Richard never had a chance to spend his Father's Day present. The bill was in his wallet when he was killed. And it was the same bill they sent to MADD.

The stains were bloodstains.

Richard Welch's family will carry forever the memory of that terrible Father's Day. And events of the days immediately following did nothing to make those memories any better.

The Welches learned that the driver who had smashed his pickup into Richard's car was a 27-year-old with three prior convictions for drunk driving! This man had no business whatsoever being allowed to drive.

A blood alcohol test administered in the hospital after the crash registered .259, nearly three times the legal limit for intoxication.

Yet, on the same day Richard Welch's wife and daughters were at the cemetery, saying goodbye to their husband and father, the man who killed him was released on a $1,000 bond—despite his prior record and the level of alcohol in his blood at the time of the crash.

Worst of all, the drunk driver never had to stand trial. The drunk driving charges against him were dropped—on a technicality. Which means he was once again free to repeat his crimes.

How did the Welches react to the news? Here's what they wrote.

"I don't understand how someone can kill a loved one and not have to pay for his crime. My husband will never get to see his daughters get married or see his future grandchildren. This man robbed him of that and us of his love and companionship."

And they didn't even have the comfort of knowing that the man who killed their husband and father would at least be prevented from destroying another family the same way he destroyed theirs.

"My fragile butterfly"

Ruth Caldwell, who founded the Pope County MADD Chapter in Russellville, Arkansas, lost her son to a drunk driver in Florida with 13 prior alcohol charges.

She tells her story:

I always used to call my son Todd my fragile butterfly. He was so gentle, so kind, so very special in every way. His music filled our home and we listened to the songs he wrote while he was with us. His dream had been to be the best rock musician in the world, a dream that he would never realize.

On the evening of December 1, 1986, the world as I knew it came to an end. I watched my husband, Mike, as he made his way to the ringing telephone in the kitchen. The expression on his face was at first blank, and then drawn, and finally shattered. He hung the phone up and walked over to tell me that there had been a car crash and that Todd had been killed.

I could not believe the words that I heard. How could this happen? No, it couldn't be true. It has to be someone else . . . no not my Todd! But it was true and our lives were changed forever.

A drunk driver with 13 prior alcohol-related charges had run a red light traveling in excess of 63 m.p.h., hitting Todd's side of the car and killing him instantly. Christopher, the small boy riding with his mother and Todd in the car was seriously injured, receiving injuries that he would carry throughout a lifetime.

Although there is a possibility now that he may not have to, we were told that he would live in an institution for the rest of his life and have to be under continual care.

As time went on, I got very angry at the Florida judicial system and their insensitivity to us. More than once it appeared that they simply weren't making much effort to do anything with Todd's case. When I flew to Florida and talked to the representative in the Prosecuting Attorney's office about Todd's case, she tried to sluff me off.

"You see all those manila file folders," she questioned as she pointed to stacks of folders on her desk. "Your son's case is just one file folder in a stack of many that need attention."

I told her that I expected something to be done soon concerning Todd's case and that Todd was more than a file folder to me.

My anger at the justice system and the desire to see something done about drunk driving led me to start a MADD chapter where I lived. I determined this was the least that I could do and that we had to start somewhere in bringing change. And, with that I called a town meeting and told my story.

People responded to what I said and we began the paperwork to organize our chapter soon after that.

When Todd's case finally came to trial, I contacted a MADD chapter in Florida. They assured me they would have people there to go to court with me. On the day of the trial, I made a request that I be allowed to speak for my son, Todd, and for Christopher and his mother, who sat holding him in the courtroom.

After I finished, the offender said that if he could he would take Todd's place. The judge responded, "Were it in my power, you would do so."

The man was sentenced to 16 years in jail and ordered to pay ten percent of any money that he might make to Christopher's mother for the next several years. It is not much, but every time he writes that check, he must surely think of the lives he has ruined and the dreams that he has destroyed. And, it's not much considering that the man only served 18 months in jail and was released.

Life without Todd has not been easy. The best that I can do most days is to survive to another day. You simply have to go on one day at a time and do the best you can on that particular day. The pain and the heartache are always there, I guess they always will be.

For all of those days that I thought that I was going crazy, I have learned that I was just coping the best way I knew how with the intense grief that filled my being. Some days I cry, lots of days I cry.

Every day I hurt as only a mother can hurt, a pain that never really diminishes because my heart is broken. A part of me is dead because a drinking driver killed my son. I feel as though someone took a claw hammer and scraped out my insides. I am empty, I am hurt, and a part of me is dead.

Throughout this experience I have learned that a time comes in the grief process that you must decide to either go on with your life or to merely go through the motions of living. It is a decision that only you can make and no one can tell you how quickly to "finish grieving" for you will grieve a lifetime in one form or another.

No one can really help, for it is only from deep within yourself that you find a reason to go on. We simply learn to go on one day at a time, that's all we can do. That's all we should be expected to do: survive one day at a time and go from there.

It Can Happen to You!

Gail Bjork told her story in the Florida State MADD Newsletter:

I don't know what woke me from my sleep at 1:30 the morning of July 25, 1987. Our bedroom door was open and I noticed the lights were still on in the living room. Our daughter Lisa, whose curfew was about midnight, hadn't turned them off when she arrived home. I got up from bed and walked in the faint light to her room. Lisa was not there.

Immediately I woke my husband Stig. We became angry that Lisa had not called as she always did whenever she was going to be late. We figured that since she had just turned 18 years old only nine days before, she had begin to flex her adult muscles and set her own hours. We paced the floor and discussed ways of punishment including taking away Lisa's car keys. Anger gradually turned to anxiety as the clock ticked on. By 2:15, I was on the phone calling and waking friends to find out where Lisa was. No one knew. By three o'clock, my husband and I decided I should go out to look for her. I pulled out of the driveway and started making a right turn onto the residential street just a few feet away from our driveway.

As I turned, I looked down the road. The early darkness was stippled with what seemed like a million blue lights. Fear gripped me as I drove a quarter mile down the street and passed through a police barricade. An annoyed policeman asked that I leave immediately. "I will, sir," I responded, "but can you please tell me if there is a young, blonde girl over there in a blue car?" The expression on the officer's face changed to anguish. He called someone on his walkie talkie. Out of the crowd came a familiar face, a local detective whom I had known for several years. "There has been a serious accident," he said. "One girl is dead." My body froze with a terror I never dreamed possible. "Is it Lisa?" I asked. "Will you be willing to make a jewelry identification?" I nodded. The detective opened his hand and my eyes fell upon the necklace her father, sister and I had given her just five weeks before for graduation. "Yes, that's Lisa's necklace. Is Lisa dead?"

I had been a concerned citizen and member of Mothers Against Drunk Driving for two and a half years before our dear daughter became a fatality and a statistic as a result of an alcohol related crash. When volunteering to fold newsletters with other members, I recall how I used to be saddened at the profound grief and agony expressed by those who had a loved one killed or injured by a drunk driver.

I had the privilege of handing Lisa her diploma on the night of June 5, 1987. I could hardly contain myself as I saw Lisa, an honor student voted by her classmates as "most likely to succeed," walking across the stage on graduation night.

Five weeks later, she was dead. William Tyler Speck of Jupiter, Florida had just left a local bar and was driving his vehicle 87-102 miles per hour in a 35 mile zone. His car hit Lisa's with such force that it split her car in two. They tell us Lisa lived for about three minutes. Speck fled, as did the three other passengers who were with him. As Speck fled, Lisa's blue eyes, robbed of their sparkle, gazed into the heavens. As he fled, a passerby held Lisa's hand until her body quivered to a halt. As he fled, a stranger tried to resuscitate her by giving CPR.

The next day newspapers reported that William Tyler Speck had amassed 13 traffic violations within the previous three years, including the suspension of his license two times. One week after he killed Lisa, his license was suspended for the third time, not related to that crash. Because Speck turned himself in 12 hours after the crash, no alcohol was found in his blood, although he admitted he had been drinking earlier that evening.

My husband seems to receive comfort when visiting our daughter's grave and, in his own way, "talks" with Lisa. When visiting her grave one day this past April, he "asked" Lisa if our family should continue its fight against drunk drivers. Five minutes after leaving the cemetery, he was hit by another drunk driver! Fortunately, there was no damage to him or our car.

The "answer," however, is one on which we all need to reflect.

"No Way on God's Green Earth"

Kevin Kirk was also victimized by a repeat offender drunk driver, suffering severe injuries himself and losing three of his best friends. Kevin's stepmom, Milo Kirk, is a member of MADD's national board of directors.

Kevin devotes a great deal of his time these days to talking to school groups about the dangers of drinking and driving. Here's his story:

On April 17, a beautiful Friday evening in Sherman, Texas, I was struck by a drunk driver. I was nine. I was a passenger in a van with members of three different families.

We were on our way to dinner and a movie when we were hit head on. I was not able to assist the others because I was unconscious.

Three friends of mine were killed in the crash. I should have been killed but was not.

I sustained a serious closed head injury and multiple internal injuries, and lost the vision in my right eye. I lay in a hospital bed unconscious for about a month.

I woke up to the fact that I lost not only my right eye and had other serious injuries, but I also lost my friend, Marshall Kendrick, a young 12-year-old boy who was talented, nice, loved and smart but now is deceased. It hurts to think about my friend. Even though we were young, I love you Marshall, as a lost brother and you will always live in my heart every single day of my remaining life.

The pain and agony I faced from losing my eye was hell, let alone waking up and telling my father I was blind in one eye. I coped with that, but to this day it is difficult to cope with the loss of a good friend. To experience a death like this in a family must be devastating.

Lucky for me I have not had that experience, but to be sitting next to your friend and in a fraction of a second lose him forever, your eye forever, and other motor functions, is devastating.

I will cherish my friends forever and those who stood by my bedside for a month to save me.

I count my blessings every day and cherish all of my future friends because there is always a possibility that I could lose them or face severe injury again.

I want to thank Mothers Against Drunk Driving for letting me tell them about my crash. I also want to commend my stepmother, who on the night of the crash was also my mom.

She is the best stepmother in the world and through her work with MADD has helped decrease drunk driving and will continue to help.

The 19-year-old who hit the van killing three people and maiming others only went to jail for two years. He had three previous DWIs and lots of other traffic violations. Even though this drunk driver served two years in jail for his ignorance and disrespect for human life, nothing will ever replace my good friend or my eye.

Hopefully, talking about it will help with some of the stress and tension I face every day.

There is no way on God's green earth that anyone should have let this man kill or the other thousands of drunk drivers kill. I hope that more people will support MADD so they won't have to wake up every day thinking about it like I do.

I will never overcome this crash as far as my pain goes, but by writing, I can let others know that we must get the drunks off the road and into jail.

Eighteen Wheels of Death and Destruction

It was a man with two prior convictions who killed Paula Standifer and five others on February 9, 1986 in a terrible tragedy that the people of Rose Hill, Kansas will never forget.

Harold Hickey's blood alcohol count was nearly twice the legal limit. Hours after the fatal crash that took six innocent lives, he still couldn't recite the alphabet.

But none of that stopped him from trying to drive a big 18-wheeler tractor trailer.

A tow truck driver would later testify that the tractor trailer passed him traveling at a high rate of speed, rocking from side to side.

The speeding truck passed several cars, showing total disregard for the ice-packed road. Then Hickey lost control, crossed the median and the truck jackknifed then collided with two oncoming vehicles.

As rescuers scrambled through the wreckage, the tragedy became painfully clear.

Four victims were from the same family, Ray Standifer, 39; his wife Marilyn "Sue," 37; Paula, 17; and Donovan, 6. Two men in the other car lay dead, too.

Other than the truck driver, the only survivors of the collision were 8-year-old Tiffanie Standifer and her 4-year-old sister Amanda.

A videotape taken of the truck driver some two hours later showed him to still be highly intoxicated. He stumbled and swayed during a sobriety test. When a state trooper asked him his age, he counted on his fingers to come up with 46. He tried twice to recite the alphabet and failed each time.

Four days before Paula Standifer would have graduated from Rose Hill High School, Hickey was convicted of six counts of aggravated vehicular homicide, driving while intoxicated, and speeding.

He immediately appealed his case on a legal technicality and plea bargaining resulted in a reduction to 5 counts of aggravated vehicular homicide.

In a sad touch of irony, Paula Standifer had helped start a Students Against Driving Drunk chapter in Rose Hill High School, and was its treasurer at the time of her death.

Known as a quiet and determined young lady, she always went about the business at hand and then moved to other things. She was an honor student with a 3.8 average and ranked third in her class. Her post-graduation plans included college and hopes for a trip to Europe.

At the Rose Hill graduation ceremonies, each member of Paula's class slipped a purple carnation into a vase on the podium which held her picture. The audience felt the pain of a requiem at what is typically the last celebration of innocence. Many bowed their heads when the public address system carried her name.

Three hours after the graduation ceremonies were

over, half of the Rose Hill senior class went to an all-night party without alcohol. The air was chilly as the teens swam, hollered and celebrated their graduation from high school.

After a while, the group gathered at a local bank to look at some videotapes of their class. They reacted to the pictures in typical teenage fashion. Group pictures taken in grade school were greeted with groans and cat-calls. Slides of cheerleaders in arched formations drew wolf whistles and cheers.

The kids were clowning around and giggling when, toward the end of the tape, pictures were shown of the school year just completed. A picture of Paula Standifer and a friend appeared on the screen and the room grew silent.

Paula's classmates watched the screen, mesmerized by the picture of the two friends arm in arm, grinning ear to ear, at a football game. For a while no one moved. No one talked. Everyone remembered.

But those students also proved that, even out of horror and tragedy, some good can come. Shortly after Paula's death, membership in the SADD chapter she helped found tripled. Plus, the school won $10,000 in scholarship money from *Reader's Digest* for the campaign they launched against drinking and driving.

It doesn't bring Paula back, and it doesn't give Amanda and Tiffanie Standifer their Mommy and Daddy and sister and brother back, but maybe, just maybe it will help save other lives.

Meanwhile, MADD continues to seek public support for its aggressive pursuit of tougher sanctions against repeat offenders, such as mandatory incarceration—confinement that cannot be suspended or probated for those convicted more than once for driving while under the influence.

A Night to Remember? Or One That Can't Be Forgotten?

Operation Prom/Graduation

The preceding chapter told the story of Paula Standifer who, along with her mother, father and brother, was killed by a drunk driver.

The story focused special attention on the reaction of Paula's classmates to her tragic death, especially on the night she would have graduated with them from high school.

Her classmates were at an all-night party. That's not unusual around graduation time. All-night parties have been around for a long time. But this was an alcohol-free party. And, until recently, that was most unusual.

The high school prom and graduation season is a very special time of year, a time for satisfaction, for the feelings of accomplishment, for celebrating the completion of one phase of a young life and beginning a new phase.

It's a time of excitement, of enthusiasm, of optimism for the future that so many bright-eyed, eager graduates feel.

It's a time of decision-making and growth.

Unfortunately, many teenagers decide to celebrate by drinking alcoholic beverages and/or using other mind-altering substances, and then getting behind the wheel of an automobile.

And what starts out as a memorable evening becomes

a memorial one.

Instead of beginning anew, life comes to an abrupt halt in alcohol and other drug-related automobile crashes.

It's become an all-too-familiar headline:

Youths Killed in Car Crash
Following Graduation Party

It is in an effort to eliminate or at least reduce that tragic loss of life during this special time that MADD has been an active supporter and promoter of Operation Prom/Graduation.

Begun in Maine in 1979 as Project Graduation, this effort has proven to be a lifesaver for thousands of high school students throughout the United States.

One of the biggest problems in addressing the drinking and driving problem among young Americans, especially teenagers, is that aura of invulnerability that surrounds us when we're young.

Young people hear all the warnings, they listen to the litany of the dangers they face, but they somehow cannot accept that those warnings, those dangers exist for them.

"That's only for the other guy, that's not going to happen to me."

Here's an English paper Brian Highland wrote on this subject for his class at Drake University.

> I recently had two good friends die in an accident because of driving under the influence of alcohol. During and after the funeral, I kept thinking to myself, "This will never happen to me." I don't know how many people told me I was lucky to be here today. After looking at my car, I think I'm pretty damn lucky myself. I learn-

ed a very valuable lesson that morning and shall never forget it.

I'm not a supporter of MADD and most likely never will be. After all, I had driven for three straight years without an accident. There were many mornings, or should I say afternoons, I woke up and was surprised to see the car parked in the driveway. I had a perfect driving record, at least up till this last month.

It was Friday night and I wanted to relieve myself from the math test earlier that day. My friend and I decided to start drinking early that night and that is exactly what we did. We went over to Peggy's to have a few draws. After slamming a few, we decided to go over to the Pike House for the all "U" party. When we reached the party, it had just started and there were very few people there. Unfortunately, that didn't stop us from drinking. As the night went on, the party picked up. People were obviously starting to catch some good buzzes. Approximately 3:30 a.m., the 12 kegs ran dry. I could honestly say that a good buzz had snuck up on me. We walked back to the dorm and relaxed for a while.

That is when I faintly remembered what the last thing my father said to me on the phone. "That car better be home early in the morning" so he could use it. My car had just gotten out of the shop about a week earlier after having approximately $600 worth of work done to it. Well, after having a hard time remembering where I parked, I finally found it and headed for home.

I was heading West on Hickman Road coming

up to the Merle Hay intersection. It was a four-lane highway in which there was a median separating the left turning lane and the lanes heading in the opposite direction. The next thing I know, there is a car pulling out in front of me. I swerved to miss the rear-end collision. I faintly remember my left front tire hitting the median. This pulled my car up onto the median which in turn slammed me head first into a 30-foot tall, 14-inch diameter aluminum pole. The next thing I remember is waking up to the lights of the police car in front of me. As I came to, I noticed that my car was in the other lanes facing the opposite direction going east. I also noticed that my head and neck was sore from hitting the windshield, and that both my knees had gone through the dashboard. Wiping the blood, which was now running down over my chin, I slowly jammed the door open and slowly got out of my trashed car.

I honestly can't tell you how I got to the back seat of the police car, but somehow I did. I don't remember if the officer asked me if I had been drinking earlier. I thought to myself when I woke up the next morning that I was very lucky because the only paper he had given me told where the car was, where the accident happened, and what time it had occurred.

Now came the fun part. Try calling your father up and telling him you totaled your car at 4:52 in the morning. All I know is that my father didn't take the news very well. The bad thing was, the car that pulled out in front of me left the scene. Besides having my insurance canceled, I am now

without a car and should soon be receiving a bill
stating how much that pole is going to cost me.

Every time a "don't drink and drive" commer-
cial came on, I laughed about it and always put it
down. Now that I think about it, those commercials are so true. Don't think that it will never
happen to you because it can and will at any given
moment. I guess I was just lucky this time, but
you never know about the next. I learned a very
valuable as well as expensive lesson that I shall
never forget.

When Brian Highland wrote that paper, he was trying to warn his fellow classmates and others about the
dangers of drinking and driving.

Unfortunately, the right person didn't hear—or at
least didn't heed—Brian's message.

He submitted his paper on November 21. Just weeks
later, three days after Christmas, Brian Highland was
dead—killed by a drunk driver.

That's why Operation Prom/Graduation is so important and why it has become one of MADD's most
visible and wide-ranging programs.

Operation Prom/Graduation helps break through
that aura of invulnerability and helps young people
learn and accept the truth about the consequences of
drinking and driving.

But we also realize at this special time of year that
education and awareness alone isn't enough. So Operation Prom/Graduation offers alternatives to today's
youngsters, alternatives like alcohol-free parties or at
the very least, free rides home from other parties.

The effort mobilizes the entire community, not only
schools and students but businesses, civic organiza-

tions, law enforcement personnel, parents and the media.

They use television and radio commercials, speakers visiting local schools, posters, fashion shows and displays in shopping malls, any means available to get the message across.

For example, MADD in Virginia joined forces with a statewide coalition that included the Virginia Department of Education, Allstate Insurance, Blue Cross and Blue Shield of Virginia, the Virginia Broadcasters Association, the Virginia Transportation Safety Administration, Pepsi Cola - East, Virginia Alcohol Safety Action Project (VASAP) and the Washington Regional Alcohol Program (WRAP).

In 1989, MADD Virginia provided more than 75,000 key tags to the graduating seniors to remind them to "Celebrate Life." Over 277 schools and organizations ordered MADD promotional materials (table tents, posters, key tags, tux-corsage cards, bumper stickers, buttons, camera-ready ads, parents' brochures and Party All Night guides) to support their local project.

The Virginia statewide group set as its goal for 1990 to have every high school in Virginia participate in the program and have an "After Prom or Graduation Alcohol-Free Party."

As Operation Prom/Graduation develops, there is a great deal of "selling" to be done, at least for the first year.

A great deal of help in that regard has come from Peter DeLuise, popular star of the hit television show, "21 Jump Street," who has been national Operation Prom/Graduation spokesperson for the past two years.

Students are "sold" on the idea that one big party will be much more fun and will offer a wider variety of activities than smaller private parties; that this may be the last time the entire class is together, it will be a night to remember and alcohol-and other drug-free seniors will be able to remember it; that they can select the activities, food and entertainment to assure that the party will be great fun for their class; and that they will be leaving a legacy of safe celebrations for undergraduates, a legacy that may well save the lives of future graduates—as well as their own.

Teachers are "sold" on the fact that all seniors will have a party to attend on graduation night; that some students will discover or rediscover what a great time they can have without alcohol or drugs; that a tradition of alcohol-free parties will be established or reaffirmed in the school district; and that the activity can enhance the school's community relations.

Lastly, parents are "sold" on the fact that no one will have to risk injury or death due to alcohol-related crashes; none of the seniors will have to deal with peer pressure to drink or to ride with a drinking driver on their special night; that, because of fund-raising activities, the cost is minimal to students and parents; and that they can relax on graduation night knowing their children are safe and having fun.

Tradition has shown that after one year of Operation Prom/Graduation, there's not a great deal of "selling" that has to be done. And the reason why that's so is the most important single fact of all about Operation Prom/Graduation:

It works!

Each year this program becomes a brighter beacon of hope as more and more states report that communities with active Prom/Graduation programs show no fatalities from alcohol or other drug-related car crashes.

That's why MADD has set as one of its goals the establishment of an Operation Prom/Graduation in every community in America.

If that happens, perhaps we will one day pick up a

national newspaper like *USA Today* and, instead of the headline mentioned earlier, read one:

Nation's Students Celebrate End of School Year:
No Drunk Driving Deaths
are Reported Anywhere!

TH!NK . . . Don't Drive and Drink!

This major multimedia public service program was developed in 1988 to serve as a complement to Operation Prom/Graduation. The "TH!NK . . . Don't Drive and Drink!" campaign is aimed at discouraging driving while under the influence of drugs, including alcohol. The program is sponsored by the Dodge Division of Chrysler Motors, Hardee's Food Systems, Goodyear Tire and Rubber Co., and PPG Industries, Inc. Nationwide in focus, it also benefits from the cooperation of the U.S. Department of Transportation, the National Association of Broadcasters and MADD.

By way of background, in 1985, the new medium of music videos was first utilized to alert Americans to the hazards of drinking and driving as Stevie Wonder's "Don't Drive Drunk" proved to be one of the most popular public service features ever made.

"TH!NK . . . Don't Drive and Drink!" was the next step in the evolution of this campaign. It was in 1988 that Aretha Franklin recorded a hot new music video version of her popular tune, "Think," with revised lyrics aimed at discouraging driving while under the influence of alcohol.

Sensing the unlimited possibilities for the fledgling campaign, the coalition took the "TH!NK" message to the streets via a national tour called "TH!NK FAST!" Local MADD chapters host the events which feature the Dodge Drunk Driving Simulator, a unique vehicle which can actually be programmed to drive drunk on a controlled slalom course. The Simulator has toured college and high school campuses.

Nicknamed by media representatives as the "MADD Mobile," the car is actually a Dodge Daytona Shelby Z equipped with a sophisticated on-board computer system which can be programmed to alter braking and steering times to correspond with a hypothetical number of alcoholic drinks consumed by the car's driver. The result is a graphic dramatization of how that person would drive after consuming the programmed number of drinks.

Still another component of the "TH!NK" program is the National Collegiate Driving Championship, an established safe-driving competition which visits up to 75 college campuses throughout the country each year, culminating in a national scholarship competition for campus winners.

Plus, the "TH!NK" campaign reaches teenagers on a mass scale through a series of four televised celebrity auto races. Popular recording artists compete at four professional road racing courses and the races are televised and syndicated to TV stations throughout the United States. Each telecast includes messages about the dangers of drinking and driving.

Operation Prom/Graduation and "TH!NK . . . Don't Drive and Drink!" are perhaps the most prominent of MADD's many programs aimed at teenagers and young adults.

And, to help break through those teenage feelings of invulnerability, consider this:

Over the past 20 years, the life expectancy in America has gone up for every age group except one—15-24 year olds. Their life expectancy has actually gone down.

The leading cause of death? Drunk driving!

Let's Save Lives!

As is readily apparent by now, MADD has many programs aimed at our young people, programs designed to create healthy, safe attitudes about the perils involved in drinking or taking drugs and then getting behind the wheel of a car.

By reaching these youngsters before they reach the legal drinking age of 21, we hope to head off life-threatening driving habits before they begin.

At the same time we focus on future drivers or beginning drivers, however, we realize all too well the need to address the habit and mindset of adult drivers.

MADD has several programs aimed at reaching those drivers as well.

Two of the most visible, Project Red Ribbon and the National Candlelight Vigil, have already been discussed. But they are only the tip of the iceberg.

Designated Driver

MADD has introduced a national Designated Driver program to help insure that only sober people get behind the wheel of a vehicle.

In a Designated Driver program, at least one individual in a group of two or more voluntarily refrains from alcohol in order to drive his or her companions home safely.

Many bars, restaurants and nightclubs in cities and

towns all across America participate in Designated Driver programs, offering free non-alcoholic beverages and other incentives to the designated driver.

The greatest advantage of the Designated Driver concept is its immediate impact. It doesn't just save lives, it keeps those lives from ever being placed at risk.

It's a familiar scene everywhere. A group of co-workers decide to stop off for a few drinks before going home.

Where it goes wrong is when one of those people who's had too much to drink gets behind the wheel of a car. That's when what started out as a simple celebration ends up a tragedy.

By having someone willing to serve as a designated driver, the group prevents that tragedy. It's as simple as that.

It's the program's simplicity that accounts for its popularity, too. A Gallup poll found that 91 percent of those who attend social functions where alcoholic beverages are served would like their circle of friends and acquaintances to adopt the designated driver plan.

And 78 percent of those who go to places or events where drinks are served said they would volunteer to act as designated drivers from time to time.

Since 1981, MADD's program has contributed to the change in America's attitudes about drinking and driving to the point where it has become easier for people, especially young adults, to choose not to drink and feel good about their decision.

A K.I.S.S. for America

Summer has become an especially dangerous time for Americans as more and more people take to the highways—and to the waterways—for adventure, relaxation, or simply a good time.

Of course, the summer holiday periods—Memorial Day, the 4th of July and Labor Day—seem to be in competition for the deadliest time of the year.

Far too many Americans never have the chance to tell "what I did on my summer vacation" because that vacation ended in death at the hands of a drunk or drugged driver or boater.

To help take some of the danger out of summer, MADD conducts a special, three-month summer program called "Keep It a Safe Summer."

MADD chapters throughout the country participate in this mammoth undertaking to help make it a success.

Informational fliers are distributed at rest areas, truck stops, sporting goods stores, convenience stores, tackle shops, marinas and every other outlet possible.

Radio and television stations broadcast public service announcements. Businesses put safe driving/boating messages on reader boards outside their establishments.

Newspapers and other print media carry information and suggestions to help promote personal responsibility for safe driving or boating.

These and other MADD programs involve as many Americans as possible in the effort to put an end to the national tragedy of drunk driving.

<u>You</u> Can Make A Difference!

Perhaps more than any other organization in the country, MADD is living proof that the drive and commitment of one person can make a difference.

This book is filled with examples of individuals and couples who chose to make a difference . . . who lit a spark which got a fire going in their communities to rid them of drinking and driving.

Here are a few other examples:

"My Needs are NOW!"
Norma Mathewson lost her son, Bill, to a drunk driver in 1985.

In 1985, when Bill was killed, there was no Mothers Against Drunk Driving in Delaware. At that time I desperately needed someone to talk to about how I felt, but no one was near. It never dawned on me to call MADD at the national level and talk to them about my grief. I began to keep a diary to help myself get through that difficult time.

Today, as I read that diary, some three years later, I am amazed at how far I have come. If anyone had told me that I would be treasurer of MADD in Delaware and then State Coordinator, I would not have believed them. I was a virtual recluse who stayed home, completely disassociating myself from friends and family. I was safe in my "cocoon" with no one to bother me.

Following is an excerpt from that diary:

THEY, whoever THEY may be, say it takes time. Only time heals the devastating pain and diminishes the anger and anguish.

It takes time to erase the painful nightmares of the tragedy and to replace them with beautiful memories of my son, Bill, memories that will make me smile rather than cry. In my mind's eye, I see Bill. I hear his laughter NOW! I can close my eyes and see his beautiful blue eyes with the mischievous twinkle in them, NOW! I want to talk to him . . . NOW! More importantly, I want to hold him NOW! And, to tell him how very much I love him NOW! Who cares about what THEY say about time and tomorrows to come. I may not be here tomorrow and future time means nothing to me. My thoughts and feelings are so intense, so urgent, my needs are NOW!

I keep running over in my mind the events that took place following Bill's death. Time and time again I return to one particular scene that keeps coming back to me, almost like I am meant not to forget it.

Place - the Medical Examiner's office. Event - we are to go down and identify Bill's body. He never made it to the hospital after the collision. As I bend down to kiss my son, I see his half-opened eye peering at me. There is no terror on his face and his eye is blank. He looks peaceful and doesn't feel my tears as I tell him how much I love him.

Later, I close my eyes and try to picture how the crash happened. I see him riding in the Jeep,

his blond hair blowing in his face. He is laughing
and having a good time. Suddenly, in a split second, the laughter turns to stark fear. I can see the
terror in his eyes as the Jeep crashes through the
trees.

The police tell me that the crash took 4 to 5
seconds. What was going through Bill's mind
during those last moments? Who and what was
he thinking of? Did his life flash before his eyes as
THEY say it does and as his life has constantly
passed before me since his death? Did he suffer
for a long time before the terror inside his head
turned into that peaceful, half-closed eye, as if he
were trying for the last time to desperately see the
world he loved and was leaving. I pray to God he
did not suffer and that the end came quickly.

It's been three years since I first wrote those
words. I still close my eyes and see Bill looking at
me. I have come to realize that I overlooked one
thing that is apparent to me now. That half-closed
eye was not haunting me, it was showing me the
peacefulness that he felt. But I could not understand it.

I think Bill was traveling through the tunnel
and saw the bright, white light of God. He knew
he was dying. He knew he was not going to be
able to live a life of quality. He did not fight death
and so he let go and was not afraid. He accepted
God's choice for him and he was at peace.

Within the past year, I realize that I have become "alive" again. My work in MADD is a constant source of therapy but more importantly, it
gave me a reason to "care" again. For a long
while it seemed incomprehensible to me that I

would ever know happiness. Now, as State Administrator for MADD, Delaware, I realize that out of the worst of tragedies, some good can come. I find that "good" in a daily personal commitment to stop drunk driving in Delaware.

"Only a Small Voice"

Thanksgiving is a time for families. Fun, food, fellowship and family gatherings. On November 30, 1980, the Thanksgiving holidays took on a new meaning for Mary Wiley and her family.

Mary Wiley was an emergency room nurse who had spent a considerable part of her life helping others. Far too often, Mary had seen the results of incidents involving drunken drivers. She had done what she could do to help people who had been injured and to comfort the families of those killed in these crashes.

Alice Wiley had come home from the University of Florida to spend the Thanksgiving holiday with her family. She was a bright, attractive young lady, with a 3.8 grade average at the university. It had been a busy time in school and she found a time to relax and rest from her studies in Bio-medical Engineering. One of her primary dreams was to design medical equipment such as kidney dialysis machines and pacemakers.

Alice and a friend had been out on a date and were returning home. A drunken driver plowed into her friend's car, throwing Alice some 83 feet from the scene of the crash. The person responsible for her death had a blood alcohol content (BAC) of .18. Alice was pronounced dead on arrival at the hospital with multiple skull fractures, thus ending her life and her dreams for the future.

Mary regrets not having been involved in the drunk

driving issue before her daughter's death. Despite seeing crash victims in the emergency room, she said she didn't understand the seriousness of the problem, "until I buried my daughter."

When Alice died, Mary's sister-in-law in Sacramento, California, asked what she could do to help. "Don't send flowers," Mary said. "Send money to a group that is working against drunk driving."

A few weeks later, Mary received a letter from the founder of MADD in California. She had received a contribution in Alice's name and added that she hoped to start MADD chapters in every state in the U.S.

With that, Mary's cause was born and she began to learn everything she could about drunk driving issues.

At first she rode with police to learn how they arrested drunk drivers in her area. She spoke extensively to judges, probation officers and prosecutors. Then she began to study the law.

In 1981, Mary Wiley began MADD in Florida and the Southeastern United States became aware of MADD's existence.

Mary decided something had to be done and she dedicated her time and energies to making a difference where she lived. "When Alice died, I didn't know which way to turn," she said. "At least people now can call us. We've all been through the same emotions."

Shortly after Mary received the letter, she showed it to an acquaintance who brushed it off with the words, "Only a small voice."

Mary Wiley proved that the voice was indeed loud and that there were other voices to join in proclaiming the message. The small voice "turned out to be a big voice. I'm surprised myself how loud."

"We CAN Change the Future"

Hal and Jane Engelke have made a family commitment to MADD. Jane is president of the Eastern Connecticut Chapter and Hal is past vice president. They have both been involved in several other positions as well. This is the story behind their involvement:

Our concern about drunk driving began in 1968 when a cousin's wife and three children were killed and a fourth child critically injured in an alcohol-related crash. Witnessing the devastation and anguish this senseless act produced made a lasting impression on us and was a frequent issue of discussion as we raised our five children.

The gravity of the issue was again brought home in 1981, when a drunk driver, unable to negotiate a turn on a winding country road, struck our car and injured me, resulting in my hospitalization. This combined with Hal's experience as an emergency room physician, motivated us to support MADD and join local efforts to put an end to this insanity through stricter laws dealing with drunk drivers and raising the drinking age. It was to be only the beginning.

On August 4, 1984, a beautiful Saturday afternoon, our youngest child, 18-year-old Thomas, was driving his girlfriend home with the promise to return for supper and a video movie. Thomas never returned. Although only 10 minutes from home, he was killed instantly and violently, and his girlfriend injured, when a drunk driver drove his car through the door of the station wagon Thomas was driving. Despite our awareness of the issue and our previous experiences, we were totally unprepared for the overwhelming pain that was to follow.

When told that Thomas had been killed, it was as though I had been struck by an overpowering blow and had fallen off the edge of the earth into a dark void. Nothing was real. There were no landmarks; no past experience that served as reference points. There was just incredible pain and emptiness. Efforts to pray were fruitless. I, to whom God had always seemed so close, believed God had abandoned me. Strangely, all I could think to say were the words of "Humpty Dumpty." The brokenness it described was what I felt. It described my helplessness; it described Thomas. It was my lament.

All through the rituals of the Church and the funeral, I kept thinking it was unreal. Somehow, if I remained controlled, I could pass this test and Thomas would return. Over and over I asked: How could this be true? How could the child we loved so dearly be dead? He was so healthy. His body, which we were now strongly advised not to view, had been perfect. He had been a gymnast. I had the medals to prove it. Everything in me rebelled against the truth and for weeks I tried to cling to my now fading belief.

Finally, the reality took hold and I confronted it. I became aware of an anger I had never known. Confused and in pain, I knew I needed help. I rummaged through the ever growing piles of sympathy notes and cards until I found the note from the newly formed, and not yet chartered, MADD chapter in our area. Now, people who had been strangers became a lifeline. They didn't tire of my story or offer simple solutions.

They, along with my surviving children, special friends, and the grace of God, helped to put "Humpty Dumpty together again."

Slowly, although forever changed, I regained strength and courage. Several months after Thomas' death, knowing I had the support of family, friends and MADD, I was able to address the court with a Victim Impact Statement. It marked the last time I was to be intimidated by others: lawyers, judges or legislators.

Hal and I both know that there is nothing that will change what has been. Justice cannot balance the scales; Thomas cannot be returned to us, but—We CAN CHANGE THE FUTURE.

With every group I address, with every drive and meeting at the legislature and every time I sit and listen to another victim's story, I recommit myself to this goal. Although, at times it is difficult and I certainly wish it were not necessary, it is what I must do. It is the best I can do.

Thomas was loved, and continues to be loved, by all of us who had the joy of knowing his gentleness, his laughter, and his smile. We give thanks to God that we were gifted with him for his short life.

Make Your Voice Heard, Too

You can make a difference, too. You can help reduce the tragedy of drunk driving in America.

There are several ways you can do that.

You can help by:

*Reporting drunk drivers promptly.

*Speaking out in your community.

*Soliciting local media to report on and inform their

audiences about the problem.

*Writing letters to the editor expressing your own concern.

*Supporting legislation to reform drunk driving laws by contacting local municipal or county elected and appointed officials, your State officials (Governor, Senator, Delegates) and your representatives at the federal level.

*Follow drunk driving cases from the law enforcement report through the judicial process in your community or county, and seek changes if necessary.

Impaired Driving Issues Program

It was the need to get maximum effectiveness from MADD's growing force of volunteer activists that led to the development of the Impaired Driving Issues Program.

In MADD's earliest actions, grief-stricken victims and their families sought to bring about change in DWI laws, their enforcement and adjudication. Those initial efforts showed the inexperience of most of the activists in dealing with the legislative process. For many it was the first visit to a legislator or the first attendance at a legislative session.

But they persevered, gradually "learned the ropes," and made their voices heard. There were marches on State Houses, attention from the media, and successes began to mount. Soon, the number of new anti-DWI bills introduced in states across the country multiplied, with more and more being enacted into law.

A major national milestone was reached in 1984 when President Reagan signed the National Minimum Drinking Age Law. MADD activists were there to cheer as the bill became law and then cheered in their own states as well when, state by state, the drinking age was raised to 21.

But as the number of volunteer activists—and the need for additional legislation—continued to grow, there was a need to provide better and more efficient training for new volunteers without demanding so much valuable time from more experienced workers.

Board member Beckie Brown, who lost a son to a drunk driver, conceived of the idea of putting together resources which could be applicable in virtually every state, to prepare new volunteers as quickly and thoroughly as possible for the legislative effort and for identifying the most important goals to pursue. Beckie's idea grew into the Impaired Driving Issues Program, an intensive program of resources and training workshops.

Through this program, aided by some highly dedicated agency officials, MADD activists and other state and community leaders learn more about each other and discuss ways to work together to put an end to the drunk driving tragedy in America.

With the first series of regional workshops held in 1988 and 1989, it didn't take long to see results. In one year: passage of administrative license revocation in four states; enactment of open container limits in Florida; and the introduction of hundreds of new pieces of legislation. The program continues to grow, with the development of additional resource volumes to further educate state leaders and MADD volunteers, as well as the general public, on the seriousness of the DWI problem and the importance of key measures to solve it.

Beckie Brown's goal, like everyone involved in MADD, is to save lives. She has worked tirelessly to assure that the Impaired Driving Issues Program does just that, by singling out countermeasures with proven value in reducing drinking and driving, incorporating them into the resources and training for the benefit of all who attend.

Support MADD's Public Policy Goals

Since 1980, there has been much progress toward tougher DWI legislation and enforcement at both the state and federal levels. However, as a new decade begins, there remains much to be done.

You can also help fight the drunk-driving tragedy in America by supporting the tougher impaired driving countermeasures necessary to win that fight—both directly and indirectly, through membership in and support of Mothers Against Drunk Driving.

MADD's mission continues to focus on two primary goals—reducing alcohol- and other drug-impaired driving, and aiding victims of crashes caused by impaired driving—but with a renewed grass-roots drive, a more organized, professional approach, and improved educational resources.

MADD is seeking, by the year 2000, a reduction in the proportion of alcohol-related traffic fatalities from the current 50 percent to 40 percent—a 10 percent reduction. We just recently launched a five year plan to help us reach that goal by addressing issues in five major areas.

Youth Issues. Reducing youthful impaired driving requires more than just raising the drinking age. In addition to its own numerous youth programs, MADD supports such measures as establishing the BAC level for underaged youth at .00, and color-coded, specially embossed drivers licenses for those under 21.

Enforcement. MADD supports the use of such effective enforcement tools as sobriety checkpoints; modern technology such as preliminary breath tests and passive alcohol sensors; per se blood alcohol content levels set at .08; and mandatory testing of all drivers involved in crashes resulting in injury or death.

Sanctions. Sanctions or penalties should serve as deterrents to discourage impaired driving as well as punishment for those offenses which do occur. Among MADD-supported sanctions are: administrative license revocation; license plate or vehicle confiscation for repeat offenses; increasingly severe penalties for repeat offenders; use of minimum-security facilities to house DWI offenders, with assessment/treatment provided as necessary; and elimination of the practice of allowing charge reduction to less serious offenses.

Self-sufficiency Programs. To insure consistent, long-term funding for comprehensive impaired driving law enforcement, MADD advocates channeling DWI fines and fees, as well as such other assessments as user fees and alcohol excise taxes, into enforcement efforts.

Responsible Marketing and Service. While never "prohibitionist," MADD has long advocated responsibility in both the marketing and serving of alcoholic beverages. MADD opposes any depiction of dangerous or illegal use of alcohol, especially promotions which target young people who cannot legally purchase alcohol. In addition, MADD opposes beverage promotions which encourage excessive consumption, such as "happy hours" multiple drink sales. Server and management training programs are advocated, since approximately half of all arrested drunk drivers are found to have been drinking in such places. Holding irresponsible establishments liable, through "dram shop" civil suits, when a patron has left intoxicated and killed or injured an innocent third party, is one way to both deter such actions and fund financial recovery for the victims.

These goals of MADD, along with other public awareness programs, seek to bring to an end the unnecessary and avoidable loss of life in our highways and streets to impaired drivers.

Here are still some other ways you can help in this all-important effort.

How to Spot a Drunk Driver

The National Highway Traffic Safety Administration offers several cues to help identify drunk drivers:

1. Turning with a wide radius.
2. Straddling the center of the road or lane marker.
3. Appearing to be drunk, i.e., eye fixation, face close to windshield, drinking in the vehicle.
4. Almost striking an object or other vehicle.
5. Weaving, or zig-zagging, across the road.
6. Driving on other than a designated roadway.
7. Swerving, or abruptly turning away from a generally straight course.
8. Driving slower than 10 mph below the speed limit.
9. Stopping without cause in a traffic lane.
10. Following others too closely.
11. Drifting, or moving in a straight-line at a slight angle to the roadway.
12. The left hand tires are consistently on the center line or lane marker.
13. Erratic braking.
14. Driving into opposing or crossing traffic.
15. Signaling that is inconsistent with driving actions.
16. Slow response to traffic signals (sudden stop, delayed start).
17. Stopping inappropriately (other than in lane).
18. Turning abruptly or illegally.

19. Accelerating or decelerating rapidly.
20. Driving with headlights off at night.

What Not to Do
1. Do not attempt to stop the vehicle.
2. Do not attempt to follow if the vehicle is exceeding the posted speed limit or if any other hazard may exist due to following the vehicle.
3. Do not disregard any traffic signals in an attempt to keep the drunk driver in view.
4. Do not follow the drunk driver too closely, because he or she may stop suddenly.
5. Do not get so engrossed in following the drunk driver that you begin weaving in the road with the drunk driver.
6. Do not attempt to detain the drunk driver if he or she should stop.
7. Do not attempt to act in the capacity of any police, fire or medical person unless you are properly trained and authorized to perform that function.
8. Do not attempt to assist a law enforcement officer while he or she is apprehending a drunk driver, unless requested.

What to Do.
Call the nearest law enforcement agency, and provide them the following information.
1. Tell them you wish to report a suspected drunk driver.
2. Give exact location (identify road and direction) of the vehicle being driven erratically.
3. Give a description of the vehicle such as model, color, license number, etc.
4. Describe the manner in which the vehicle is being

driven.

**Thirty Simple Things You Can Do to Stop
Drinking and Driving in America**

START BY GETTING THE FACTS STRAIGHT!

1. Understand that alcohol, wine, and liquor are drugs.

2. Understand that the word "drunk" means being visibly impaired, such as staggering, slurring speech, etc.

3. Understand that "intoxicated" is a legal term reflecting the amount of alcohol in a person's blood. In most states, a blood alcohol content of .10 percent is required to be convicted of drinking and driving. In some states it is .08 percent.

4. Understand that "impaired" means that your ability to think clearly and to react appropriately are not fully functional.

5. Understand that you can be "impaired" by alcohol and other drugs long before you become "intoxicated" or "drunk."

6. Understand that research shows that your ability to drive is "impaired" at a .04 to .05 percent blood alcohol content. (American Medical Association)

7. Understand that at low levels of intoxication, you can "feel" more competent to drive than you did before beginning to drink. This is a false security.

8. Understand that cold showers, coffee, or exercise will not hasten the lowering of your intoxication level. Only time can do that—and alcohol burns off much more slowly than it is consumed.

9. Understand that in every state in the nation, drunk driving is now a crime.

10. Understand that getting behind the wheel only once when your ability to drive is impaired could change your life forever.

CHANGE THE WAY YOU TALK!

11. Stop saying "alcohol and drugs" and start saying "alcohol and other drugs."

12. Stop saying "accident" when referring to incidents caused by impaired drivers. It wasn't accidental. It resulted from two clear choices — one, to use alcohol or other drugs, and two, to drive. Start saying "drunk driving crash" or "drunk driving crime."

13. Stop saying, "If all my kids use is alcohol, I'll be happy!" Start saying, "I don't want you to use alcohol until you're 21 because it's against the law."

14. Stop laughing at jokes — and telling jokes — which take impairment or intoxication lightly.

15. Stop ignoring lack of clarity when your children talk about "partying." Ask what it means and encourage alcohol and other drug-free socializing.

16. Stop saying "one for the road" and start saying "none for the road."

17. Practice saying "No, thank you" when offered a drink until you can do it comfortably.

18. Say, "No thanks, I'm driving" when you plan to drive.

19. When alcohol ads are clearly designed to reach the "under-21" age group, point out their inappropriateness to those who view them with you.

20. Say "yes" when a MADD volunteer asks for your support.

WINNING THE WAR BEGINS AT HOME!

21. Never drink and drive, regardless of your age.

22. Begin now (if you haven't already) to designate a driver <u>before</u> you leave the house, if your outing involves drinking. It will cement the idea in your child's mind.

23. Build your child's self esteem by discussing in advance how compromising situations might be handled. Praise your child for seeking internal control and demonstrating external control.

24. Start educating your child with the truth about alcohol and other drugs <u>early</u>. If you don't, someone else will.

25. Teach responsibility at an early age. After your child starts driving, insist that he or she pay at least part of the insurance premium and all of any traffic tickets received.

26. Refuse to serve alcohol to any child, including your own, until they are 21.

27. If you see evidence that your child has been using alcohol or other drugs, confront it immediately.

28. If your child needs professional help, don't be too embarrassed to get it.

29. If you need professional help, don't be too embarrassed to get it.

30. Walk like you talk—then you will have nothing to be ashamed of.

Solving the drunk driving problem in America begins at home.

You can make a difference. Get involved in America's drunk driving problem. Please.